AGAINST ELECTIONS

Congo: The Epic History of a People

DAVID VAN REYBROUCK

Against Elections

The Case for Democracy

introduction by
Kofi Annan

TRANSLATED BY
LIZ WATERS

Seven Stories Press
new york • oakland

Seven Stories Press
140 Watts Street
New York, NY 10013
www.sevenstories.com

Library of Congress Cataloging in
Publication Control Number: 2017051901

Printed in the USA

1 3 5 7 9 8 6 4 2

The people of England deceive themselves when they fancy they are free; they are so, in fact, only during the election of Members of Parliament: for, as soon as a new one is elected, they are again in chains, and are nothing.

Jean-Jacques Rousseau,
The Social Contract (1762)

Contents

INTRODUCTION

The Crisis of Democracy *by Kofi Annan*   ix

I   SYMPTOMS

Enthusiasm and mistrust: *The paradox of democracy*   1

Crisis of legitimacy: *Support is crumbling*   5

Crisis of efficiency: *Declining vigour*   10

II   DIAGNOSES

It's the fault of politicians: *The diagnosis of populism*   17

It's the fault of democracy: *The diagnosis of the technocracy*   20

It's the fault of representative democracy: *The diagnosis of direct democracy*   24

It's the fault of electoral-representative democracy: *A new diagnosis*   37

III PATHOGENESIS

A democratic procedure: *Drawing lots
(antiquity and Renaissance)*   58

An aristocratic procedure: *Elections
(eighteenth century)*   78

The democratisation of elections: *A bogus
process (nineteenth and twentieth centuries)*   92

IV REMEDIES

The revival of sortition: *Deliberative
democracy (late twentieth century)*   106

Democratic innovation in practice:
An international quest (2004–2013)   115

Democratic innovation in the future:
Allotted assemblies   131

Blueprint for a democracy based on sortition   138

Timely appeal for a bi-representative system   150

Conclusion   163

Acknowledgements   167

Bibliography   172

Notes   179

Index   193

The Crisis of Democracy[1]
by Kofi Annan

Let me start by invoking the name of Aristotle, one of the most enduring thinkers Greece, and indeed the world, has ever produced. His very name means "excellent insight," and he certainly left us quite a few, which continue to resonate more than 2,000 years after his death. Not least is Aristotle's recognition that "Man is, by nature, a political animal." Man is born, lives and dies as a member of a community and the affairs of that community are therefore his, and vice-versa. I am honoured to speak in his name and, as you will see, I believe many of his insights are as relevant today as they were in antiquity.

I have been a tireless defender of democracy all my life because I am convinced it is the political system most conducive to peace, sustainable development, the rule of law and the respect for human rights, the three pillars of any healthy and democratic society. As the UN Secretary General, I oversaw the creation of Democracy Day and the UN's Democracy Fund, to support grassroots democracy around the world. Since leaving the UN, I

---

1 This introduction was adapted from a speech made by Kofi Annan at the 2017 Athens Democracy Forum on 13 September 2017. Printed here by permission of Kofi Annan.

have set up the Electoral Integrity Initiative with a group of concerned organizations and individuals who seek to promote the legitimacy of elections as a fundamental pillar of democratic practice. The Kofi Annan Foundation and its partners have just held regional conferences in Latin American and Southeast Asia, which highlighted the challenges democracy faces in those regions, but also peoples' commitment to its ideals.

We have to admit that democracy is experiencing a crisis of confidence. Not only does it face increasingly assertive opponents, but growing numbers of its beneficiaries either take it for granted, or else doubt its merits. Much has been made of reports by Larry Diamond, of the Economist Intelligence Unit and Freedom House, that democratic freedoms have been in retreat for eleven straight years in many parts of the world, with the emergence of an increasing number of elected authoritarians. But even in democracy's historic heartlands, we are witnessing a shift in the perceptions and practice of democracy evidenced by ever lower levels of voter participation, falling membership of political parties and declining trust in politicians and institutions. According to Pew, less than a fifth of the American population trust their federal government to "do the right thing most of the time." It used to be three fourths in 1958. The U.S. Congress, for its part, has a 69% negative rating. This is based on the perception that democracy isn't delivering. Governments appear powerless in the face of face of such challenges as the Euro crisis, the migration crisis, or the debt crisis.

Elections have become almost universal since the end of the Cold War. Yet in many countries where elections are held, freedom and democracy are actually in retreat. Intended as mechanisms for the peaceful arbitration of political rivalries, they frequently become flashpoints for political violence. At the core of these paradoxes are elections without integrity. All too often, elections serve merely to give autocratic regimes a veneer of legitimacy. But elections without integrity cannot provide the winners with legitimacy, the losers with security and the public with confidence in their leaders and institutions. This makes polities fragile as it encourages disgruntled groups to find other, less constructive, channels for the expression of their discontent.

This has set the scene for the resurgence of populism—charismatic individuals or fake prophets promising simplistic solutions to people's grievances through radical policies that dismiss institutions and laws as either irrelevant or inconvenient.

What are the factors driving these challenges to democracy? I see at least three.

First, growing inequality within countries. The uneven benefits of globalization are dividing societies into winners and losers on an unprecedented scale. Global markets are creating billionaires, whilst the incomes of the middle and working classes in developed countries have stagnated and their livelihoods are becoming ever more vulnerable to technological change and global competition. Compounding inequality, increasingly integrated financial markets have allowed globalization's footloose winners to park their profits in tax havens, while the tax burden on the middle class continues to rise. Aristotle himself stressed the importance of the middle class for the sustainability of democracy. When wealth is too concentrated, the polity becomes vulnerable to oligarchy. If there are too many poor, the polity can degenerate into populism, disorder and the confiscation of private property. The middle class is the backbone of a democracy and Aristotle advocated that it should always far outnumber both the poor and the rich. The threat to the middle class is therefore a threat to our political systems themselves.

Second, governments are looking increasingly powerless in the face of the imperatives of the global economy and the ever-growing web of regional and global agreements they have entered into. In Greece, for example, the inability of Syriza to overturn the EU's austerity policies despite the party's popular mandate to do so no doubt created a sense of disillusionment. I think that the management of the 2008 Great Recession has increased suspicions that democratic governments have been captured by special interests. Whilst the US government was spending trillions in bailing out the big banks, for example, millions of American families lost their homes. In Greece, there is a widespread perception that the EU prioritized the protection of the big European banks' balance sheets over the protection of the Greek population, whose incomes fell by about a third. We are not here to debate the economic arguments of the decisions that were made, but I think the political price of those priorities was high.

Finally, there is a crisis of effectiveness. Democratic government is compared unfavorably with the concurrent success of authoritarian regimes, which seem to enjoy record rates of growth. Whilst the US government's plans to overhaul its infrastructure have been stuck in Congress for almost a decade, China has built the Three Gorges Dam and thousands of miles of new railways and roads. People—especially in developing countries that are struggling to overcome poverty and low growth—look at these achievements and wonder whether democratic governance, at least in its Western incarnation, really delivers.

These are all real and serious problems that we cannot dismiss, lest the populists of both left and right continue to gain ground. Be that as it may, we need to put these concerns into historical perspective. The setbacks of the last decade have to be set against remarkable gains since the end of the Second World War, when there were only twelve fully-fledged democracies. Today there are 117, and elections, however flawed, have become almost universal, illustrating the power of legitimacy they offer.

We should not forget that liberal democracy almost died in the 1930s, but the liberal democracies eventually defeated Nazism, Fascism and Communism. Democracy is therefore arguably the most successful political system the world has ever seen. Polls show that most people around the world aspire to more freedom, more rule of law, more accountability and more say in politics. In short, democracy remains a universal aspiration.

Why? Because it actually delivers. Of the twenty countries with the highest levels of human development as measured by the UN's human development index, nineteen are liberal democracies. Among the top forty, thirty-six are liberal democracies. And even the citizens of poorer democracies live, on average, nine years longer than citizens of poor autocracies, because they have better access to health and education. Democracies are also less vulnerable to famines and conflicts. Most importantly, however, as my friend Amartya Sen has cogently argued, freedom itself is development. Subordination to the caprices of other human beings, rather than to the law, is a source of despair to the human soul.

I am skeptical about the sustainability of "authoritarian growth." In most cases, both historically and globally, those regimes become fragile when growth slows or ends, because they have no other sources of legitimacy. So rather than looking for alternatives to liberal democracy, we should instead seek to reform our systems through concrete measures in at least three areas.

First, we need to make our democracies more effective. Much of the debate in our democracies turns on the politics of redistribution and public spending, but not enough on effectiveness. We are trying to solve today's problems with yesterday's solutions. We must harness new technologies and management techniques to overhaul the administration of the state to make our democracies less bureaucratic and more responsive to families and individuals, especially those who cannot afford high-priced lawyers and lobbyists.

Second, we need to tackle inequality, both economic and political. As I have said, increasing inequality is one of the drivers of resentment, especially since economic inequality leads to political inequalities as well, as several studies have confirmed. There is a growing perception that the priorities of the extremely wealthy take precedence over the wellbeing of the middle class thanks to campaign contributions and lobbying. At the other end of the spectrum, the poor and minorities are, or at least feel, excluded from the political system. Governments must respond by redistributing fairly the benefits of globalization by restricting tax avoidance and evasion schemes, and most importantly, discouraging tax havens. Fortunately, democracy is one of the only systems in which the concerns of the majority can overturn the interests of the wealthy if the majority harnesses the mechanisms at their disposal. But this demands more participation, not less.

This means that we need to make our democracies more inclusive. This requires bold and innovative reforms to bring in the young, the poor and minorities into the political system. An interesting idea put forward by one of your speakers this week, Mr. David Van Reybrouck, would be to reintroduce the ancient Greek practice of selecting parliaments by lot instead of election. In other words, parliamentarians would no longer be nominated by political parties, but chosen at random for a limited term, in the way many jury systems work. This would prevent the formation of self-serving and self-perpetuating political classes disconnected from their electorates.

Third and finally, we need to champion democracy. The victory over Nazism, fascism and Communism were also ideological struggles that were won on the battlefield of ideas as well. Yet many of the tools of that battle have been abandoned or are underfunded today. Democracy's enemies are spending billions to undermine it, both in practice and through misinformation. In a world of "alternative facts," who do we believe? We know that armies of state-financed trolls are creating "AstroTurf movements" to sow the seeds of mistrust and disunity to weaken our democracies. We must not let them win by abdication. Democracies have to reclaim the lost ground by defending and promoting liberal ideas, just as they did against democracy's past ideological enemies.

Athenian democracy illustrates that practice never meets the ideal–women could not vote and slavery was common practice. Moreover, ancient Athenian democracy was sometimes hijacked by oligarchics, reminding us that democracy is vulnerable. We should remember that democracy is always a work in progress. But a system created thousands of years ago continues to inspire democrats throughout the world today. We must cherish, reform and defend democracy, or else it may be lost for future generations. As another great democrat who drew inspiration from ancient Athens, Thomas Jefferson, put it, "the price of liberty is eternal vigilance."

I

Symptoms

Enthusiasm and mistrust: The paradox of democracy

There is something strange going on with democracy. Everyone seems to want it but no one believes in it any longer, even though international statistics tell us that more and more people say they're in favour of it. A few years ago the World Values Survey, a large-scale international research project, questioned more than 73,000 people in fifty-seven countries, representing almost 85% of the world's population. When asked whether they believed democracy to be a good way of governing a country, no fewer than 91.6% answered in the affirmative.[1] The proportion of the global population that has a positive attitude to the concept of democracy has never been as great as it is today.

This degree of enthusiasm is nothing short of spectacular, especially in light of the fact that less than seventy years ago democracy was in a very bad way. As a result of fascism, communism and colonialism, when the Second World War ended there were only twelve fully fledged democracies.[2] Slowly the number started to rise and in 1972 there were forty-four free states.[3] By

1

1993 they numbered seventy-two and now there are 117 electoral democracies out of a total of 195 countries, ninety of which can actually be defined in practice as free states. Never before in history have there been so many democracies, never before so many supporters of this form of government.[4]

Yet enthusiasm is declining. That same World Values Survey showed that worldwide over the past ten years, there has been a considerable increase in calls for a strong leader 'who does not have to bother with Parliament and elections', and that trust in parliaments, governments and political parties has reached a historical low.[5] It would appear that people like the idea of democracy but not the reality of it, or at any rate not the current reality.

This reversal can be attributed in part to the new democracies. Twenty years after the fall of the Berlin Wall, disillusionment in many countries of the former Eastern Bloc has become particularly marked. The Arab Spring does not appear to have heralded a democratic summer and even in countries where elections have been held (Tunisia, Egypt), many people are discovering a darker side to the new order. For those who experience democracy for the first time it is sorely disappointing to discover that in practice democracy is often a less than ideal system, especially when democratisation is accompanied by violence, corruption and economic decline.

But that is not the only explanation. Even convinced democrats are afflicted by feelings of uncertainty and nowhere is this paradox more striking than in Europe. Although the concept of democracy has historical roots here and can still rely on mass support, trust in the actual institutions of democracy is visibly declining. In the autumn of 2012, Eurobarometer, the European Union's official research bureau, noted that only 33% of Europeans still have faith in the European Union. (In 2004 the figure was 50%.) Faith in their own national parliaments and governments was even lower at 28 and 27% respectively.[6] These figures are some of the lowest in years, an indication that today, two-thirds to three-quarters of people distrust the most important institutions of their political ecosystems. Although a certain scepticism is an essential component of critical citizenship, we are justified in asking how widespread this distrust might be and at what point healthy scepticism tips over into outright aversion.

Recent figures give the impression that a general distrust pervades public life in Europe, not confined to formal politics but also encompassing public services, such as postal deliveries, healthcare and the railways. Faith in politics is part of a broader experience, but if we look specifically at democratic institutions, then it's clear that political parties meet with the greatest distrust of all (they score an average of 3.9 out of 10 among EU citizens), followed by governments (4 out of 10), parliaments (4.2 out of 10) and the press (4.3 out of 10).[7]

The distrust is mutual, incidentally. In 2011 Dutch researcher Peter Kanne presented some interesting figures on how politicians in The Hague look at Dutch society. A full 87% of the country's governing elite sees itself as innovative, freedom-loving and internationally oriented, but 89% think the Dutch are generally traditional, nationalistic and conservative.[8] So politicians assume that, on the whole, citizens adhere to other, in their view lesser, values than they do and there's no reason to believe that the picture is different elsewhere in Europe.

However, getting back to the citizen, the reason often given for this increase in distrust is the 'apathy' which results from individualisation and consumerism. This is said to dull citizens' critical engagement to such an extent that their faith in democracy has subsided into half-heartedness. At best they now bob about in listless indifference and change channels the moment politics is mentioned, having given up, we are informed, on politics. That, however, is not entirely in accordance with the facts, as while it may be true that a substantial proportion of people have little interest in politics, that has always been the case. There has been no recent decline, in fact research shows that concern about political issues is greater than it used to be and people discuss such issues with friends, family and colleagues more than they did in the past.[9]

This interest in politics is not a reason to feel reassured, however, as an era in which interest in politics grows while faith in politics declines always has something explosive about it. After all, it means there's a growing gulf between what citizens think and what they see politicians doing, between what they regard as vital and what in their view the state is neglecting, resulting in a build-up of frustration. What does it mean for the stability of a country if more and more people warily keep track of the doings of an authority which they increasingly distrust? How much derision can a system endure? And is it still merely derision, now that everyone can express and share their deeply felt opinions online?

We live in a world quite opposite to that of the 1960s. Then a simple farmer and his wife could be completely apathetic about politics and yet have complete faith in democracy.[10] Sociological research confirms such confidence existed, a faith that characterised large parts of Western Europe. Then there was apathy and trust while now there is passion and distrust. These are turbulent times.

Crisis of legitimacy: Support is crumbling

Democracy, aristocracy, oligarchy, dictatorship, despotism, totalitarianism, absolutism and anarchy: every political system has to achieve a balance between two fundamental criteria, efficiency and legitimacy. Efficiency is all about how quickly a government can find successful solutions to problems that arise, while legitimacy is about the degree to which people give their assent to the solution.

To what degree do the people recognise the authority of the government? Efficiency is about decisive action while legitimacy is about support, the two criteria usually existing in inverse proportion to each other. A dictatorship is undoubtedly the most efficient form of government (one person decides and that's it) but it rarely enjoys much lasting legitimacy. The reverse, a country that engages in endless consultation with all its residents, no doubt nurtures support for the government, but at the expense of its ability to act.

Democracy is the least bad of all forms of government precisely because it attempts to find a healthy balance between legitimacy and efficiency, resulting in criticism sometimes of one side, sometimes of the other. The system keeps itself upright like a captain on the deck, shifting his weight from one leg to the other to ride with the swell, but today Western democracies are struggling with a crisis of both legitimacy and efficiency, a highly unusual situation. This is no longer a heaving sea but a raging storm and to make sense of it we have to look at figures that rarely make the front pages. If we carry on staring through a magnifying glass at the ripples of every opinion poll or election result, we'll lose sight of the bigger picture, the great ocean currents and weather patterns.

In what follows I examine national governments in a number of countries. Obviously there are also local, regional and supranational echelons, each with its own dynamics and reciprocity, but the national level best lends itself to a broad investigation of the health of representative democracy.

Three unmistakable symptoms denote the crisis of legitimacy. First, fewer people are voting. In the 1960s more than 85% of Europeans took part in elections. In the 1990s the figure was less than 79% and in the first decade of the twenty-first century it fell below 77%, the lowest since the Second World War.[11]

In absolute numbers, this means millions of Europeans no longer wish to use the ballot box and they represent a quarter of those entitled to vote. In the US the trend is even more pronounced. Voter turnout at presidential elections is less than 60% and at midterm elections only around 40%, figures which indicate that electoral absenteeism is fast becoming the most important political movement in the West, even though we never hear about it. In Belgium the legal obligation to vote keeps the absenteeism figure rather lower (at around 10% on average over the past ten years), but it has risen, from 4.91% in 1971 to 10.78% in 2010.[12] Despite massive media coverage of the Belgian local council elections in 2012, turnout was the lowest in forty years and in cities such as Antwerp and Ostend, absenteeism came close to 15%.[13] The figure for Antwerp is particularly astonishing, considering that the battle for the mayoral sash dominated the national media for months. In the Dutch parliamentary elections of September 2012, no fewer than 26% of those eligible to vote stayed home.[14] These figures are telling when compared to 1977, when only 12% of citizens declined to vote.[15] Democracy has a serious problem of legitimacy if citizens no longer wish to take part in its most important procedure by going to the polling station. Is it still possible to claim that Parliament represents the people? Shouldn't a quarter of seats be left empty for four years?

Second, alongside low voter turnout we are seeing high voter turnover. Those qualified to vote in Europe not only vote less, they are more capricious. Those who do vote may still recognise the legitimacy of the procedure, but they show less and less loyalty to a particular party. The organisations set up to represent them receive only provisional support from the electorate and in this context political scientists speak of 'electoral volatility' and conclude that it has increased enormously since the 1990s. Figures suggest a turnover of 10, 20 or even 30%, resulting in the rule of the floating voter and an increasing incidence of political earthquakes. 'The elections that have so far taken place in the new century confirm this trend,' a recent synthesis claims. 'Austria, Belgium, the Netherlands and Sweden have gone on to new record highs, with the sudden growth in support for the far right (in the Netherlands in 2002) or its sudden decline (in Austria in 2002) producing election outcomes that rank among the most volatile in western European history.'[16]

Third, fewer and fewer people are members of a political party.[17] In EU member states less than 4.65% of those eligible to vote hold a party membership card. On average, that is. In Belgium 5.5% still have a party card (as opposed to 9% in 1980), in the Netherlands only 2.5% (as against 4.3% in 1980), but the steady decline is unmistakable everywhere. A recent scientific study called the phenomenon 'quite staggering' and after systematic analysis, researchers concluded:

> In extreme cases (Austria, Norway), the decline is greater than 10%; in others, it is around 5%. All cases, with the exception this time of Portugal as well as Greece and Spain, also record a major long-term decline in the absolute numbers of members. There is a drop of 1 million or more in Britain, France and Italy, around half a million in Germany, and close to that in Austria. Britain, Norway and France have lost well over half their party members since 1980, while Sweden, Ireland, Switzerland and Finland have lost close to half. These are genuinely striking figures, and suggest that party membership as such has, in general terms, changed in both its character and its significance.[18]

What does it mean for the legitimacy of the democratic system that so few people ally themselves with the most important players within it? How much does it matter that political parties are the most distrusted institutions in Europe? And why do the leaders of those parties so rarely lose sleep over the fact?

Crisis of efficiency: Declining vigour

There is not only a crisis of democratic legitimacy, efficiency too is heavily strained. Effectual government has become more and more difficult, and sometimes a decade and a half might pass before parliaments actually vote on a law. It's getting harder to form a government, coalitions are often less stable than in the past and they are punished increasingly harshly by voters when their term ends. Elections, in which fewer and fewer people take part, often make governments less efficient. Let's look again at three symptoms.

First, coalition negotiations are taking longer than ever, especially in countries where complex alliances are needed. After June 2010, Belgium broke all records by going without a government for a year and a half, but during the past few years in Spain, Italy and Greece too, a long and laborious process has been required to form a government after elections. Even in the Netherlands the situation is becoming more difficult. Of the nine coalitions in the post-war period that took more than eighty days to form, five date from after 1994.[19] The reasons for this are many and varied, and one reason certainly is that coalition agreements are becoming longer and more detailed. This is a remarkable evolution if one considers that times are more unpredictable than ever and flexible anticipation of acute needs is the order of the day. But it seems that so great is the distrust between coalition partners, and so great the fear of being punished by voters, that every small point of policy has to be firmly nailed down. Every party wants the best achievable deal, everything must be set in stone beforehand and it's all about arriving home and dry with as much of the party programme intact as possible. Inevitably, this means a long period of negotiation.

Second, parties in government are coming under increasing attack. Comparative research into representative governments is a fairly young science, but some of the results are striking and that is certainly true of research into electoral 'payback' in Europe. What is the fate of a governing party at the next election? In the 1950s and 1960s, parties that joined a coalition government lost 1 to 1.5% of their votes, in the 1970s 2%, in the 1980s 3.5% and in the 1990s 6%. Since the start of this century the figure has been 8% or more. In recent elections in Finland, the Netherlands, Britain and Ireland, governing parties lost 11, 15, 15 and 27% of their voters respectively.[20] Who still wants to govern proactively in Europe if the price of participation in government is so relentlessly high? Standing on the sidelines is a much more rational choice at the moment, certainly if it has no effect on party financing, such as in systems where the state pays.

Third, government is a slow business these days. Large infrastructure projects such as the new metro line in Amsterdam, the new station in Stuttgart, the motorway around Antwerp or the new international airport at Nantes are sometimes completed only with great difficulty, if at all. National governments in Europe have lost much of their prestige and power, tied as they are to dozens of local and supranational players. If such projects used to be a source of prestige and knowledge, they are now at best a governmental nightmare. The proud era of the Delta Works, the Afsluitdijk, the TGV network and the Channel Tunnel is over. If even building a bridge or a tunnel is no longer achievable, what can national governments still do under their own steam? Very little, as it happens, because they are bound hand and foot by the national debt, European legislation, American rating bureaux, multinational corporations and international treaties. In the twenty-first century, sovereignty, once the basis of the nation state, has become a relative concept. This means that the great challenges of our day – climate change, banking crises, the euro crisis, economic crises, offshore fraud, migration, overpopulation – can no longer be dealt with adequately by national governments.

Powerlessness is the key word of our time: the powerlessness of the citizen in the face of government, the government in the face of Europe and Europe in the face of the world. Everyone looks down at the mess below and then looks up, no longer with hope and faith but with despair and anger. Power today is a ladder on which everyone stands and curses.

Politics has always been the art of the possible and now it has become the art of the microscopic. The inability to address structural problems is accompanied by the overexposure of the trivial, fuelled by our insane media that, true to market logic, have come to regard the exaggeration of futile conflicts as more important than any attempt to offer insight into real problems, especially in times of falling media revenues. The fact that ephemeral obsessions dominate as never before is a phenomenon studied by the Dutch parliament in 2009. It betokens a great deal of self-awareness that the steering group for parliamentary self-reflection wrote in its report:

In order to survive the next election, politicians try to score again and again. The increasingly commercialised media are all too happy to offer them a podium, so these three sectors [politics, media and business] have each other in a hold, a Bermuda Triangle that by some mysterious means pulls everything down, with everyone wondering why it happens . . . The interaction between politics and the media certainly seems to be an important factor in creating more and more incidentalism in politics. Media live by news. In our conversations with journalists it was noted that incidents are better at attracting media attention than good debates, which also occur.[21]

In this connection 'incidentalism' is a useful word and the figures leave no room for doubt. Over recent years the number of verbal questions, written questions, motions submitted and emergency debates in the Dutch parliament has shot up, in parallel with the frequency of political talk shows on Dutch television, because a parliamentarian needs to score once the cameras are running. 'Members of Parliament would rather be "astonished", "shocked" and "extremely unpleasantly surprised",' wrote one of those who provided information for the report. 'In the nineteenth century there may perhaps have been too many elderly lawyers in the Lower House; nowadays there are too few.'[22]

If eagerness to promote an image wins out over governing, if election fever becomes a chronic disorder, if compromise is consistently described as treachery, if party politics systematically evokes contempt, if participation in government is guaranteed to lead to heavy electoral defeat, why would an idealistic young person go into politics? Parliamentary anaemia threatens and the recruitment into politics of new, passionate people is getting harder – a secondary symptom of the efficiency crisis. Politics as a profession is going the same way as teaching, once a noble calling that commanded respect, now a lousy job. A Dutch brochure about enlisting new political talent has a title that speaks volumes: *Finding and Keeping*.[23]

Retaining political talent is far from simple and it burns up more quickly than it once did, as Herman Van Rompuy noted when he was president of the European Council. 'The way in which our democracies work wears people out at a terrifying rate. We have to take care that democracy itself doesn't wear out.'[24]

This goes to the heart of the efficiency crisis. Democracy has become comparatively toothless but at the same time noisier. Instead of sitting mumbling to themselves in a corner, disconcerted by their own impotence, modest about their limited room for manoeuvre, today's politicians can, indeed must, shout their virtues from the rooftops – elections and the media leave them no choice – preferably with fists clenched, legs stiff and lips together, since that looks good and makes them appear effective. Or so they think. Instead of meekly recognising that the balance of power has changed and going in search of new and more worthwhile forms of government, they keep on playing the electoral-media game, often against their own best interests and those of the citizens who are starting to find it all a bit tiresome and whose trust is not likely to be won back by so much overwrought and transparent hysteria; the efficiency crisis only exacerbates the crisis of legitimacy.

The results are predictable and the symptoms exhibited by Western democracy are as manifold as they are vague. Anyone who puts together low voter turnout, high voter turnover, declining party membership, governmental impotence, political paralysis, electoral fear of failure, lack of recruitment, compulsive self-promotion, chronic electoral fever, exhausting media stress, distrust, indifference and other persistent paroxysms sees the outlines of a syndrome emerging. Democratic Fatigue Syndrome is a disorder that has not yet been fully described but from which countless Western societies are nonetheless unmistakably suffering. Let's look at the diagnoses that already exist.

II

Diagnoses

THE AVAILABLE ANALYSES of Democratic Fatigue Syndrome could be seen as falling into four diagnostic categories: it's the fault of politicians, it's the fault of democracy, it's the fault of representative democracy and – one specific variant – it's the fault of electoral-representative democracy. I'll look at them in that order.

It's the fault of politicians: The diagnosis of populism

That politicians are careerists, money-grabbers and parasites, that they're profiteers, that they're out of touch with the common man and that we'd be better off without them. The slogans are familiar enough and populists make use of them daily. According to their diagnosis, the crisis of democracy is first of all a crisis of political personnel and our current rulers form a democratic elite, a caste completely divorced from the needs and grievances of the average citizen. No wonder democracy is in trouble!

It's a discourse that in Europe is verbalised by seasoned leaders such as Silvio Berlusconi, Geert Wilders and Marine Le Pen, but also by relative newcomers such as Beppe Grillo in Italy, Norbert Hofer in Austria, and parties such as Jobbik (Hungary), the Finns Party (previously known as the True Finns) and Golden Dawn (Greece). In the English-speaking world we have seen the spectacular rise of figures like Nigel Farage and, of course, Donald Trump. According to them the remedy for Democratic Fatigue Syndrome is relatively simple: better representation of the populace, or rather more popular representation of the populace, preferably in the form of a larger vote for their own populist parties. The leaders promote themselves as direct representatives of the people, as the voice of the underbelly, the embodiment of common sense. They claim that unlike their colleagues they are close to the man or woman in the street, that they say what they think and do what needs to be done, and that the populist politician is at one with the people.

That all this is questionable in the extreme we know well enough, because there's no such thing as one monolithic 'people' (every society has its diversity), nor is there anything that could be described as a 'national gut feeling', and common sense is the most ideological thing imaginable. After all, 'common sense' is an ideology that refuses to recognise its own ideological character, like a zoo that sincerely believes it is an example of unspoilt nature. The notion that someone can be at one with the masses in some organic way, at one with their values and unfailingly conscious of their fickle yearnings, is a belief that tends more towards mysticism than politics: no deep current exists, only marketing.

Populists are political entrepreneurs trying to gain as large a market share as they can, if need be by deploying a little romantic kitsch. It is unclear how, once they have gained power, they intend to deal with those who think differently, since democracy gives power to the majority while retaining respect for the minority – otherwise it degenerates into a dictatorship of the majority that will make us even worse off.

Deploying populism as a solution to the sickness of democracy is therefore not a promising path to take. But that the remedy doesn't work is not to say it cannot possibly offer some valuable assistance.[25] Populists are right, in that those who today maintain they represent the people do indeed have a problem with legitimacy. The number of highly educated people in our parliaments is so out of proportion that we would be right to speak of a 'diploma democracy'.[26] Moreover, there is a recruitment problem. Representatives were once chosen 'because they meant something in society', as sociologist J.A.A. van Doorn put it. Now, even among populists, we see more and more 'professional politicians, often young people with more ambition than experience. They are going to mean something because they've been elected.'[27] No less problematic is the tendency to regard the role of being a Member of Parliament as an interesting career, a full-time job sometimes passed on from father to son, rather than a temporary service lasting just a few years and performed for the sake of society. In Flanders several democratic dynasties have emerged and we are already into the second generation of the families De Croo, De Gucht, De Clercq, Van den Bossche and Tobback. Brand awareness speeds the journey to Parliament, 'while some wouldn't even have made it onto the local council with another name', as a former top politician once told me, off the record.

Simply dismissing populism as a form of anti-politics seems to me intellectually dishonest. At its best populism is an attempt to tackle the crisis of democracy by increasing the legitimacy of representation. Populists want to combat Democratic Fatigue Syndrome by means of one simple but drastic intervention; fresh blood in Parliament, a blood transfusion, as complete as possible, and the rest will take care of itself. Opponents wonder whether this will do anything to increase efficiency and doubt if government will improve because a few new people have been taken on board. To them the problem is not the people who staff our democracy but democracy itself.

It's the fault of democracy: The diagnosis of the technocracy

Democratic decision-making which has become slow and long-winded undermines belief in the democratic process, and faced with the huge and urgent challenges of, for example, the euro crisis, the search is on for a more efficient system. An obvious solution would appear to be technocracy, a system where experts are charged with looking after the public interest, people whose technical know-how will pilot the country through today's troubled waters. Technocrats are managers who replace politicians, so they don't need to worry about elections but can concentrate on long-term solutions and announce unpopular measures. In their hands policy becomes a matter of civic engineering, of problem-management.

It's often thought that those who advocate technocracy are the concerned elite who want to see progress. But is it really a question of populism for the people, technocracy for the elite? In fact research in the US has shown that ordinary people have a fairly casual attitude to the prospect of giving power to unelected experts or entrepreneurs: 'People would rather thrust power at someone who does not want it than someone who does,' note the authors of the influential *Stealth Democracy*. Most citizens want democracy to be like a Stealth bomber: invisible and efficient. 'Successful business people and independent experts, though not necessarily empathetic, are perceived to be competent, capable individuals not in pursuit of power. That is enough for many people, or at least it is better than the kind of representation they believe they are receiving now.'[28]

The argument for technocracy builds to an important degree on the 'post-political' thinking of the 1990s. In that era of the Third Way in politics, of the *Neue Mitte* and *la cohabitation*, there was a belief that ideological differences were a thing of the past. After decades of conflict, left and right suddenly walked arm in arm. The solutions were there, people said, they only had to be implemented and it was simply a matter of 'good governance'. Ideological struggle gave way to the TINA ('there is no alternative') principle, and the foundations for a technocratisation of politics had been laid.

The most striking recent examples of such a turn towards technocracy are to be found in countries like Greece and Italy, where in recent years unelected leaders have been allowed to head government teams. Loukas Papadimos was in power from 11 November 2011 to 17 May 2012, Mario Monti from 16 November 2011 to 21 December 2012. Their financial and economic expertise (one as a banker, the other as an economics professor) were seen as trump cards when the crisis was at its worst.

But technocracy comes about in countless other less visible places. In recent years a huge amount of power has moved from national parliaments to transnational institutions such as the European Central Bank, the European Commission, the World Bank and the IMF. Because these are not democratically elected, they represent a far-reaching technocratisation of decision-making: bankers, economists and monetary analysts have got their hands on the levers of power.

This is not just about foreign organisations. Every modern nation state has given itself a technocratic slant by removing competences from the democratic arena and depositing them elsewhere. The power of central banks and constitutional courts, for example, has grown markedly. It seems governments have thought it sensible to take crucial tasks such as monetary supervision and constitutional reform out of the clutches of party politics and the electoral calculus that goes with it.

Is this a bad thing? There is no doubt that a technocratic government can achieve great results, the Chinese economic miracle being the best example, while a leader like Mario Monti was a far better manager of public affairs than Silvio Berlusconi could ever be. But efficiency does not automatically generate legitimacy and faith in the technocrat melts away as soon as spending cuts are implemented. In the presidential elections of February 2013, Monti won only 10% of the vote. China has its own ways of suppressing dissatisfaction with government-by-regents.

There is little point in regarding technocracy as taboo, if only because new states often start out with a technocratic phase, as for example the Fifth Republic of Charles de Gaulle in 1958 or Kosovo in 2008. A state does not always emerge by democratically legitimate means and after a revolution power is always in the hands of an unelected elite for a transitional phase. The trick then is to organise elections or a referendum as quickly as possible, so that the trust-gauge can start rising and legitimacy can be created *a posteriori*. In the short term a technocracy can give fresh impetus, in the long term it is not a viable form of government. Democracy is not just government for the people but government by the people.

Technocrats work in precisely the opposite way to populists. They try to relieve Democratic Fatigue Syndrome by giving efficiency priority over legitimacy in the hope that good results will eventually win the approval of those they govern, in other words, in the hope that efficiency will spontaneously generate legitimacy. That may happen certainly, but politics is more than simply a matter of good government. Sooner or later, moral choices have to be made, choiccs which require consultation with society. But where can such a consultation take place? 'In Parliament' is the standard answer, but it is an answer which many are beginning to question and which brings us directly to a third diagnosis.

It's the fault of representative democracy: The diagnosis of direct democracy

On 2 August 2011, twelve people sat in a circle in Bowling Green Park in New York City.[29] That day was the high point of one of the most astonishing episodes in recent American history. Over the preceding weeks and months Democrats and Republicans had been unable to agree about raising the American debt ceiling.[30] The Democrats wanted the government to borrow more on international money markets to ensure the nation kept working, whereas the Republicans would agree to that only if President Obama also made a huge saving by reducing federal expenditure on those most in need of care. The Republicans, stirred up by the Tea Party, dug in their heels saying: cuts first, and only after that our fiat. The Democrats, who thought minimal taxation for the richest fairer than draconian cuts for the poorest, refused to bow to Republican blackmail. In any case the vast American national debt had been created by the Republicans, with their senseless military intervention in Iraq.

The debate reached total deadlock and the day was rapidly approaching on which, according to calculations, the American government would no longer be able to pay its bills and salaries: 2 August 2011. It was rather like a tactical standstill in cycling, when the leading riders balance almost at a halt just before the finish – if neither side makes a move, they'll soon be overtaken by the peloton. A huge economic recession would overtake the US, and there was even the threat of a worldwide crisis, since if the treasury of the largest economy on the planet were to run out of money, the rest of the world would be dragged down with it. It got to the point where even technocratic China asked democratic America not to go too far as party interests were all well and good, but there was such a thing as statesmanship. In the end the Democrats were forced to back down and the Republicans emerged victorious. It was as if the 2012 presidential campaign was already well under way.

The twelve in Bowling Green Park were totally fed up with the course of events. The insane tug of war between two parties had come within a hair's breadth of casting the entire world economy into a crisis. Was Congress still the environment in which representatives of the people served the public interest, or were the House of Representatives and the Senate more a playground for two parties playing childish games of increasingly reckless speculation? One of those present was a Greek artist who lived in New York.[31] She proposed not merely protesting but using a method she had seen in Athens, that of a 'general assembly' in a public space which random passers-by could join, and be given a chance to speak. Points of view were expressed on both sides and the entire group sought a consensus. That experience of egalitarian, direct democracy, as an alternative to the wrangling of representative democracy, proved infectious. The meeting in Bowling Green became bigger and bigger in the months that followed, and Occupy Wall Street was born.

The reference to Wall Street and the slogan 'We are the 99%' suggest that the movement was all about the economy, but in reality dissatisfaction with representative democracy lay at the root of the protest.[32] One of the participants put it like this:

> In Congress, there is a claim that there is the united goal of serving the American people, but in reality there is a power war between political parties. Also, our elected representatives are not reflecting the perspectives of all their constituents. They are only representing the perspectives of those in their preferred political party and the monied elite who fill their campaign coffers – in reverse priority of course. This gets to the core complaint of the 99%. Our representatives aren't representing us.[33]

The Occupiers who camped out for weeks in Zuccotti Park in the autumn of 2011 took their inspiration from demonstrators on Tahrir Square in Cairo and the Puerta del Sol in Madrid. A general assembly was held twice a day, a kind of parliament outside Parliament, a political forum without political parties, where citizens could put forward any proposals and discuss them without having to go through elected representatives. The general assembly lay at the heart of the movement and it quickly developed its own arsenal of rituals, most striking among them the 'people's mic'. Because amplification was banned, everything was acoustic, without technical aids, even at meetings with many hundreds of participants. A person would speak and the people around would repeat what they said until the message reached those right at the back in a series of waves. To express agreement or disagreement or to ask for further elucidation, various hand signals were invented. The meetings had no chair, no leaders of factions, no spokespeople, at most a few moderators to keep the process on track. Horizontality was the name of the game.[34]

It led to the emergence on 23 September of the 'Principles of Solidarity', the movement's first official document. Principle number one was not about casino capitalism, globalisation, bonus culture or the banking crisis, but about democracy. As a response to a sense of political disenfranchisement, the item that headed the list was 'Engaging in direct and transparent participatory democracy'.[35]

Elsewhere in the Western world, people took to the streets in search of a better democracy. In Spain the Indignados grew into a major movement with 'Real Democracy Now' as its slogan. On Syntagma Square in Athens tens of thousands of Greeks shouted slogans in favour of true democracy at the doors to the parliament building. The Beurs van Berlage in Amsterdam, the London Stock Exchange and the European Central Bank in Frankfurt found people camping outside their doors. In Germany there were the Wutbürger, angry citizens protesting against the new station in Stuttgart, night flights over Frankfurt, a third runway at Munich and the transport of nuclear waste by rail; 'Wutbürger' was chosen as word of the year in 2010. In Belgium I was one of those present at the start of the G1000, which campaigned for more citizen involvement in political decision-making. In cyberspace we all watched the rise of Anonymous and the Pirate parties.

In December 2011 *Time* magazine chose the protestor as its personality of the year and shortly after that the London School of Economics devoted a broad international study to the sudden rise of all this subterranean politics in Europe. The results are of great significance:

> The most important finding that emerges from our project is that what is shared across different types of protests, actions, campaigns and initiatives is extensive frustration with formal politics as it is currently practiced. The terms 'angry', 'indignant' or 'disappointed' are an expression of this frustration . . . German society is far less affected by austerity measures than other European societies . . . Yet, despite the relatively positive situation in Germany, there is a striking public display of subterranean politics in Germany just as in other European contexts. This is because current protests are not so much simply about austerity but about politics.[36]

It is clear that many of those protestors consider Democratic Fatigue Syndrome the result of our current representative democracy, with its decaying structures and rituals. They agree with the technocrats that contemporary democracy has many faults, but they don't want to replace it with something else, as the technocrats advocate: they want to improve it. How? Certainly they do not believe that injecting new people into parliament, as the populists suggest, is a solution. A blood transfusion is not a guaranteed cure for a body that is at death's door. Moreover, they are not as enamoured of the cult of the leader as are the populists: it's far too vertical for them, and it remains a form of delegation. What, then? The efficiency of the technocrats doesn't appeal to them either. Their own peculiar, roundabout way of conducting meetings shows that they regard legitimacy as a good deal more important than rapid results.

If you take a close look at Occupy Wall Street and the Indignados, what is striking is the movement's strong anti-parliamentarianism. 'Our representatives aren't representing us,' they said in New York while in Madrid it was put like this:

In Spain most of the political class doesn't even listen to us. Politicians ought to hear our voice and make political participation by citizens possible by a direct route, so that society as a whole is involved, instead of thriving at our expense and focusing all their attention on the dictatorship of big economic powers.[37]

Occupiers and Indignados feed on adjectives: new democracy, deep democracy, horizontal, direct, participative, consensus-driven democracy. In short they hunger for true democracy and believe that parliaments and parties have had their day. They set consensus against conflict, consultation against voting, respectful listening against theatrical quarrels. They refuse to have leaders, make no concrete demands and distrust the outstretched hand of existing movements. When the Indignados marched through the streets of Brussels, flags of political parties and even trade unions were unwelcome. Those were all considered to be part of the system.

The last time we saw such vehement anti-parliamentarianism in Europe was between the wars. Because the First World War and the crisis of the 1920s were commonly seen as the outcome of nineteenth-century bourgeois democracy, three leaders inveighed bitterly against the parliamentary system: Lenin, Mussolini and Hitler. Nowadays it is often forgotten, but fascism and communism were originally attempts to make democracy more vital, based on the idea that if parliament was abolished, the people and their leader would be better able to converge (fascism) or the people could govern directly (communism). Fascism quickly degenerated into totalitarianism, but for quite some time communism continued to seek new forms of collective consultation. It is worth dusting off Lenin for a moment. In his famous *State and Revolution* of 1917, he advocated dispensing with parliamentarianism, noting that 'Parliament is given up to talk for the special purpose of fooling the "common people"'. He conveyed Marx's view of the process of holding elections in a sentence that would not have been out of place in New York or Madrid: 'The oppressed are allowed once every few years to decide which particular representatives of the oppressing class shall represent and repress them in Parliament.' For the development of his alternative he took inspiration from the Paris Commune of 1871 (the source of the word 'communism'):

> The Commune substitutes for the venal and rotten parliamentarism of bourgeois society institutions in which freedom of opinion and discussion does not degenerate into deception . . . Representative institutions remain, but there is no parliamentarism here as a special system, as the division of labour between the legislative and the executive, as a privileged position for the deputies.[38]

That some supporters of the Occupy movement compare the occupiers of Zuccotti Park with the Paris Commune is a relatively minor fault; pathos can overcome the best of us.[39] But that a movement which lashed out so fiercely against the parliamentary system had no knowledge of history and had given no thought to viable alternatives was not just a strategic weakness, it was downright foolhardy. Was it truly aiming at a complete defeat of the existing model, and if so how were we to see the future? What guarantees were there of equality and freedom? How could we avoid making disastrous mistakes? It's really not enough to be likeable and unconventional if you're going to tinker with something as crucial as the consultative model. The great French philosopher of democracy Pierre Rosanvallon was right to warn that 'When efforts are undertaken to make democracy stronger, it can turn against itself and become totalitarian, as happened in the Soviet Union'.[40]

When Slovenian philosopher Slavoj Žižek spoke to the Occupiers in New York, he asked them not to fall in love with themselves, but unfortunately that is exactly what happened. In a damning essay, American journalist Thomas Frank describes how the movement became devoted to the cult of participation, of 'direct democracy', and how the means became an end in itself:

Building a democratic movement culture is essential for movements on the left, but it's also just a starting point. Occupy never evolved beyond it. It did not call for a sub-treasury system, like the Populists did. It didn't lead a strike (a real one, that is) or a sit-in, or a blockade of a recruitment centre, or a takeover of the dean's office. The IWW free-speech fights of a century ago look positively Prussian by comparison. With Occupy, the horizontal culture was everything. 'The process is the message,' as the protesters used to say.[41]

Dutch sociologist Willem Schinkel adds: 'Occupy is in a sense the simulation of ideological resistance. The desire for a counter-ideology is central to it, far more so than any actual counter-ideology.'[42]

Occupy demonstrates the malaise more than it suggests any remedy. Its diagnosis of representative democracy was correct, but the alternative was weak. For participants in the general assemblies it will undoubtedly have been a moving and enjoyable experience, as the sense of being part of a community that discusses things in a calm and adult manner can be extraordinarily intense. There can never be too much cultivation of civic virtues, especially when parliament and the media no longer set a good example. But how that process might be extrapolated to echelons that can truly make a difference was unfortunately never explored. Stéphane Hessel, the French diplomat and former resistance hero whose pamphlet *Indignez-vous* gave a name to the Indignados, stressed repeatedly that indignation without engagement is not enough and that real attempts to influence governments are needed: 'We must not become engaged at the margins but at the heart of power.'[43]

*

Each of the three remedies I have discussed so far appears to be dangerous, in that populism endangers the minority, technocracy endangers the majority and anti-parliamentarianism endangers freedom.

But in Europe in recent years a number of other movements have emerged that are not satisfied with symbolic protest at the margins. They have truly sought to reach 'the heart of power' and their members might be dubbed 'neo-parliamentarians'. The Pirate Party, which emerged in Sweden in 2006 and which in Germany, virtually at least, was briefly the third largest party, is one of them. In the Netherlands the G500 tried by artful means to break into the main political parties and the Dutch Parliament. And Beppe Grillo's Five Star Movement grew to become the third largest party in Italy.[44]

What is striking about these neo-parliamentarian movements is that they aimed to strengthen representative democracy by adding new forms of consultation. The Pirate Party evolved from a platform for digital rights into a political movement that wanted to enrich democracy with direct democracy.[45] With the G500 more than five hundred young Dutch people suddenly became members of the three large parties of the centre so that they could influence their party manifestos. Later they invited voters to give more weight to their votes through the Stembreker (vote-breaker) by grouping their votes strategically. Here too the aim was to increase consultation, both within parties and in the formation of governing coalitions.

Despite its leader's populist rhetoric, the Five Star Movement aimed to improve the representation of the people by imposing new rules: no representatives with criminal records, no seats for life, no election of the same person for more than two terms. This was intended to open the door to allow more participation in politics by ordinary citizens.

Another striking aspect of these three initiatives is that after a rapid start and an avalanche of media attention, the enthusiasm of the public and the media quickly ebbed away and what at first seemed vivacious and new was put out with the trash after just a few months. Being elected to parliament does not give you authority as far as the media are concerned. You have four years to grow into the job of representing the people, but from the first day after the election you need to score immediately on the radio, preferably with wisecracks and familiarity with all that has gone before, as if you've never done anything else in your life. Amateurism is great, as long as it's not amateurish. Even before you've been able to reveal your plans you're written off; talents and ideals quickly burn out as a result. The new movements are certainly admirable for not turning their backs on parliament, but in today's society, where perception is everything, winning an election is by no means enough.

Yes, Democratic Fatigue Syndrome is caused by the weakness of representative democracy, but neither anti-parliamentarianism nor neo-parliamentarianism will turn the tide, as neither has properly investigated the notion of representation. One rejects it, the other still believes in it, but both unquestioningly assume that the representation of the people in a formal consultative organ is inextricably bound up with elections. We need to take a closer look at that assumption.

It's the fault of electoral-representative democracy: A new diagnosis

In recent years, countless suggestions have been made with regard to strengthening representative democracy and reinstating its old glory, and they mostly take the form of new rules. An example would be that those who fulfil a political function must not combine their public office with their private sector work, or they must declare their income and wealth, or political parties must be financially transparent and comply with stricter requirements before they can receive government subsidies, or they must make their archives accessible to all, and so on. Or, finally, new rules for elections have been suggested, stating that national, regional and European elections must fall on the same day so that a quiet period can follow, constituencies be redrawn, methods of counting votes rethought and electoral rolls expanded. Shouldn't parents be able to vote on behalf of their children, for example, so that they can indicate their long-term preferences? Shouldn't it be possible to vote for several parties at the same time, so that the 'particracy' is reduced? Shouldn't votes for ideas (referendums) be given a permanent place alongside votes for people?

All these proposals are helpful, some perhaps necessary, but even if they were all fully implemented, the problem would not be entirely solved, because Democratic Fatigue Syndrome is caused not by representative democracy as such but by a specific variant of it: electoral-representative democracy, the democracy that produces a body of representatives through elections. This requires further elucidation.

The words 'elections' and 'democracy' are nowadays synonymous for almost everyone. We have become convinced that the only way to choose a representative is through the ballot box. After all, the Universal Declaration of Human Rights of 1948 states as much: 'The will of the people shall be the basis of the authority of government; this will shall be expressed in periodic and genuine elections which shall be by universal and equal suffrage and shall be held by secret vote or by equivalent free voting procedures.' That 'shall be expressed' is symptomatic of our way of looking at the issue: to say democracy is to say elections. But is it not remarkable that such a general document – the most universal legal document in human history – defines so precisely how the will of the people must be expressed? Is it not bizarre that a concise text about basic rights (fewer than two thousand words in total) pays attention to the practical execution of one of them, as if legislation about public health were to include a recipe? It's as if the people who compiled the declaration in 1948 had come to see the specific method as a basic right, as if the procedure was in itself sacred.

It would appear that the fundamental cause of Democratic Fatigue Syndrome lies in the fact that we have all become electoral fundamentalists, despising those elected but venerating elections. Electoral fundamentalism is an unshakeable belief in the idea that democracy is inconceivable without elections and elections are a necessary and fundamental precondition when speaking of democracy. Electoral fundamentalists refuse to regard elections as a means of taking part in democracy, seeing them instead as an end in themselves, as a holy doctrine with an intrinsic, inalienable value.

This blind faith in the ballot box as the ultimate base on which popular sovereignty rests is seen most vividly of all in international diplomacy.[46] When Western donor countries hope that countries ravaged by conflict, like Congo, Iraq, Afghanistan or East Timor, will become democracies, what they really mean is this: they must hold elections, preferably on the Western model, with voting booths, ballot papers and ballot boxes, with parties, campaigns and coalitions, with lists of candidates, polling stations and sealing wax, just like we do, only over there, and then they will receive money from us. Local democratic and proto-democratic institutions (village meetings, traditional conflict mediation or ancient jurisprudence) stand no chance. These things may have their value in encouraging a peaceful and collective discussion, but the money will be shut off unless our own tried and tested recipe is adhered to – rather in the way that traditional medicine must back off as soon as Western medicine turns up.

If you look at the recommendations of Western donors, it's as if democracy is a kind of export product, off the peg, in handy packaging, ready for dispatch. Democracy becomes an Ikea kit for 'free and fair elections', to be put together by the recipient, with or without the help of the instructions enclosed.

And if the resulting piece of furniture is lopsided, uncomfortable to sit on or falls apart? Then it's the fault of the customer, not the distant producer.

That elections can have all kinds of outcomes in states which are fragile, including violence, ethnic tensions, criminality and corruption, seems of secondary importance, and that elections do not automatically foster democracy but may instead prevent or destroy it is conveniently forgotten. We insist that in every country in the world people must traipse off to the polling stations, no matter how much collateral damage may result. Our electoral fundamentalism really does take the form of a new, global evangelism. Elections are the sacraments of that new faith, a ritual regarded as a vital necessity in which the form is more important than the content.

*

This focus on elections is actually rather odd. For almost three thousand years people have been experimenting with democracy and only in the last two hundred have they practised it exclusively by holding elections. Yet we regard elections as the only valid method. Why? Force of habit is at play here, of course, but there is a more fundamental cause, based on the fact that no one can deny that elections have worked pretty well over the past two centuries. Despite a number of notoriously bad outcomes, they've very often made democracy possible and they've brought order to the laborious quest for a credible balance between the contrasting demands of efficiency and legitimacy.

However, what is often forgotten is that elections originated in a completely different context from that in which they have to function today. Fundamentalists generally have little historical insight, assuming their own dogmas always held good, and electoral fundamentalists therefore have a poor knowledge of the history of democracy. This is orthodoxy without retrospection. In fact we badly need to take a look back.

When the supporters of the American and French revolutions proposed elections as a way of getting to know 'the will of the people', there were as yet no political parties, no laws regarding universal franchise, no commercial mass media, let alone social media. In fact the inventors of electoral-representative democracy had no idea that any of these things would come into existence. Figure 1 shows how much the political landscape has evolved since then.

There was a time when Europe had no citizens, only subjects. From the Middle Ages until well into the eighteenth century – here we are painting with a broad brush – power lay with a sovereign ruler, excepting the Dutch, Florentine and Venetian republics, which we will leave aside for now. In his palace, fort or castle, the ruler, perhaps with the help of a few nobles or councillors, took decisions about the affairs of his country. His decisions were conveyed to the market square by a messenger, who announced them to anyone willing to listen. The relationship between power and the masses was a one-way street, and this remained the case from feudalism to absolutism.

But over the course of the centuries a 'public sphere' emerged, to borrow a phrase and a theory from German sociologist Jürgen Habermas. Subjects resisted the top-down approach and gathered in public to discuss affairs of state. In the eighteenth century, the century of enlightened despotism, events gathered momentum. Habermas has described how places developed where people could discuss public matters. In Central European coffee houses, at German *Tischgemeinschaften*, in French restaurants and British pubs, the affairs of the day were debated. The public sphere took shape in new institutions such as

FIGURE 1: Elections in historical perspective: the main developments in the electoral-representative system in Western democracies

Before 1800

From the era of feudalism to the era of absolutism, the aristocracy was in charge. Power lay with the sovereign, whose authority was ascribed to divine origins. Supported by the nobility (knights, courtiers), he dictated the laws. There was no public sphere.

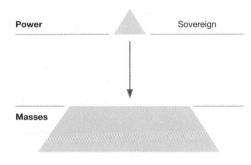

1800

The American and French revolutions limited the power of the aristocracy and established elections to give a voice to popular sovereignty. Authority no longer came from above but from below. The right to vote remained confined to the top echelons of society. Public debate took place mainly in newspapers.

1870-1920

Two crucial evolutionary processes occurred everywhere: political parties emerged and universal suffrage was adopted. Elections became a battle between diverse interest groups, which attempted to represent as large a proportion of society as possible.

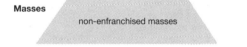
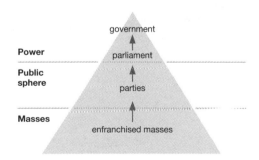

43

1920-1940

The economic crisis of the interwar years placed representative democracy under great strain. Here and there the fuses blew. There were experiments with new political models, the most significant of which were fascism and communism.

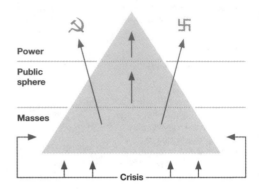

1950

Representative democracy recovered miraculously. Power was in the hands of large political parties, which were in close contact with citizens through a jumble of mediating organisations such as unions, corporations, sometimes educational networks and the parties' own media. Party loyalty was firm, voting habits predictable. Mass media (radio and television) were in the hands of the state.

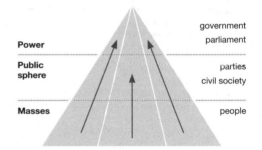

1980-2000

Two decisive developments: organised civil society foundered and commercial media gained power. The electoral system lost stability as a result. The more the public sphere was filled by private players (and even public media began to follow the logic of the market), the more party loyalty declined. Political parties shifted from the core of civil society to the outer shell of the state apparatus. Elections became a fierce media battle for the favour of the floating voter.

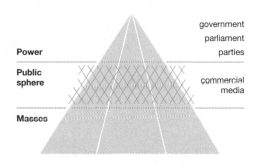

2000-2020

Social media and an economic crisis are bringing further difficulties for representative democracy. New technology gives individuals a voice, but this only places yet more pressure on the electoral contest: the campaign is now permanent. The work of government suffers from electoral fever, the credibility of those in government suffers from their need to stand out. Since 2008 the financial-economic crisis has been throwing oil on the fire. Populism, technocracy and anti-parliamentarianism are flourishing.

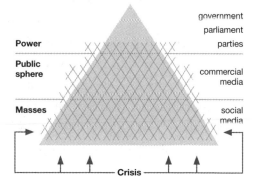

cafés, theatres, opera houses, but perhaps most of all in that peculiar invention of the time, the newspaper. The political awareness that emerged during the Renaissance came to characterise larger and larger groups. The citizen was born.

The American and French revolutions of 1776 and 1789 represent the high point of this development. A rebellious citizenry threw off the yoke of the British and French crowns and decided that the people were sovereign, not the king. To give the people a voice (or at least the bourgeois segment of the population, since the franchise was still very limited), a formal procedure was invented, the election, a procedure until then mainly used to choose a new pope.[47] Voting was familiar as a means of achieving unanimity among a group of like-minded people, such as cardinals, but in politics it would now have to promote consensus between people seen as virtuous within their own circles. For a citizen of the early twenty-first century it takes a certain amount of imagination to conceive of a time when elections were not there to produce arguments but to promote unity. The public space par excellence – the place where individuals could speak in complete freedom for the sake of all – was called the parliament. Edmund Burke said of it: 'Parliament is not a congress of ambassadors from different and hostile interests; which interests each must maintain, as an agent and advocate, against other agents and advocates; but parliament is a deliberative assembly of one nation, with one interest, that of the whole.'[48] Even Jean-Jacques Rousseau, with whom Burke disagreed on countless matters, was of the same opinion: 'In proportion to the degree of concord which reigns in the assemblies, that is, the nearer opinion approaches unanimity, the more the general will predominates; while tumults, dissensions, and long debates declare the ascendancy of private interests and the declining situation of the State.'[49] Parliamentarianism was the late-eighteenth-century citizenry's answer to the absolutism of the *ancien régime*. It stood for a form of indirect, representative democracy. The enfranchised 'people' (meaning the bourgeois elite) chose its representatives and those representatives promoted the public interest in parliament. Elections, representation of the people and press freedom went hand in hand.

Over the next two centuries, this eighteenth-century method went through five structural transformations; political parties arose, universal suffrage was introduced, organised civil society grew, commercial media drowned out the public arena and social media added their voices to the clamour. It goes without saying that the external economic context is of great relevance too, as in times of crisis enthusiasm for democracy ebbs away (in our own time between the wars) whereas in times of prosperity the tide rises again.

Political parties emerged only after 1850. Of course there were already fault lines in the young democracies, such as between city-dwellers and provincials, between the money-rich and the land-rich, between Liberals and Catholics or between federalists and anti-federalists. But only towards the end of the nineteenth century did these groups evolve into clearly defined, formal groupings. There were still no mass parties, only executive parties with a modest number of members and the ambition to govern, but this soon changed, and although most constitutions do not mention them at all, they quickly became the most important players on the political pitch. Socialist parties, for example, became the greatest advocates of universal suffrage. Its introduction (in 1917 in the case of Belgium and the Netherlands, in 1918 in the United Kingdom, although in each case only for men) represented a structural transformation of the electoral system. Elections became a battle between different interest groups in society, each trying to gain the support of as large a segment of the electorate as possible. Elections, originally intended to promote unanimity, now became arenas for candidates who fought each other fiercely. The clash of the parties had begun.

After the First World War, love of electoral democracy cooled markedly. The economic crisis of the 1920s and 1930s fragmented support and anti-parliamentary, totalitarian models gained in popularity all over Europe.

No one could have suspected that after the worldwide conflagration of 1940–45, democracy would flourish again, but the after-effects of the war and the enormous growth in prosperity of the 1950s and 1960s made many people in the West receptive to a reintroduction of the parliamentary system.

In the post-war years large mass parties dominated, and they held the structures of the state in their hands. Through a network of intermediary organisations (unions, corporations, state-controlled health services, even school networks and their own party media) they succeeded in being close to the lives of individual citizens. The public sphere was largely in the hands of this organised civil society. Governments owned the biggest and newest mass media (radio and television), but parties were able to participate through directorships, broadcasting slots or their own broadcasting organisations. All this resulted in an extremely stable system with great party loyalty and predictable voting behaviour.

The equilibrium came to an end as a result of neo-liberal thinking, which reshaped public space radically in the 1980s and 1990s. Not civil society but the free market was now the main architect and this applied to countless domains of public life, especially the media. Party newspapers disappeared or were bought up by media concerns, commercial broadcasters entered the field and even public broadcasters increasingly adopted market thinking. There was a true explosion of media. Viewing, reading and listening figures became hugely important; they were the daily share price index of public opinion. Commercial mass media emerged as the most important builders of social consensus and organised civil society lost ground, whether because unions and state health services adopted a market model or because governments preferred to talk to citizens directly rather than via social partners. The consequences were predictable, as citizens became consumers and elections hazardous. Parties, especially when they were financed largely by governments (often to limit the risk of corruption) saw themselves less and less as intermediaries between the masses and power and instead settled into the fringes of the state apparatus. To retain their places there they had to turn to the voter every few years to top up their legitimacy and elections became a battle fought out in the media for the favour of voters. The passions aroused among the populace diverted attention from a far more fundamental emotion, an increasing irritation with anything and everything pertaining to politics. 'It would be hard to find someone who wasn't cynical about the nature of these media-corporate spectacles that are presented to us as elections,' said American theoretician Michael Hardt a couple of years ago.[50] 'Elections are just a beauty contest for ugly people,' was the sarcastic comment doing the rounds on the internet.

In 2004 British sociologist Colin Crouch came up with the term 'post-democracy', to describe the new order controlled by the mass media:

> Under this model, while elections certainly exist and can change governments, public electoral debate is a tightly controlled spectacle, managed by rival teams of professionals expert in the techniques of persuasion, and considering a small range of issues selected by those teams. The mass of citizens plays a passive, quiescent, even apathetic part, responding only to the signals given them. Behind the spectacle of the electoral game, politics is really shaped in private by interaction between elected governments and elites that overwhelmingly represent business interests.[51]

The Italy of Berlusconi undoubtedly comes closest to fitting the definition of the post-democratic state but elsewhere too we have seen processes that tend in that direction. Since the end of the twentieth century, citizens have started looking like their nineteenth-century predecessors. Because civil society has become weaker, a gulf has opened up again between the state and the individual. The channelling institutions have gone. Who now bundles the multiplicity of individual preferences? Who now translates grass-roots complaints into policy proposals at the top? Who now distils the tumult into clear ideas? There is pejorative talk of 'individualism', as if it's the fault of the citizen that collective structures have fallen away, while in essence this is all about the fact that the people have become the masses again, the choir a cacophony.

It's not over yet. After the rise of the political parties, the introduction of universal suffrage, the rise and fall of organised civil society and the coup by commercial media, another factor was added at the start of the twenty-first century: social media. The word 'social' is rather misleading, since Facebook, Twitter, Instagram, Flickr, Tumblr and Pinterest are as much commercial media as CNN, FOX or Euronews, with the difference that the owners don't want you to watch and listen but to write and share. Their main aim is to keep you on the site for as long as possible, since that's good for the advertisers. This explains the importance attached to 'friends' or 'followers', the addictive dynamics of 'likes' and 'retweets', the continual stream of reports on what others are doing, whom you ought to get to know and which topics are trending.

But although social media are commercial media, they have a dynamism very much their own. At the beginning of the twenty-first century citizens could follow the political theatre minute by minute on radio, television or the internet but today they can respond to it from second to second and mobilise others. The culture of immediate reporting now has instant feedback resulting in even more of a cacophony. The work of the public figure, and especially the elected politician, is not made easier by any of this. He or she can immediately see whether new proposals appeal to the citizen, and indeed just how many people the citizen can whip up. New technology gives people a voice (allowing Mubarak and Ben Ali to join the conversation), but this new political involvement only makes the electoral system creak at the seams all the more.

Commercial and social media also reinforce one another; continually picking up each other's news and bouncing it back, they create an atmosphere of perpetual mud-slinging. Tough competition, loss of advertising revenue and falling sales prompt the remaining commercial media to produce increasingly vehement reports about increasingly exaggerated conflicts, while their editorial boards become smaller, younger and cheaper. For radio and television, national politics has become a daily soap, a radio play with free actors, and while editors determine to some extent the framing, the script and the typecasting, politicians, with varying degrees of success, try to slant things this way or that. The most popular politicians are those who succeed in altering the script and reframing the debate, in other words bend the media to their will. There is space for some improvisation, which is then called topicality.

In the written press the entanglement is even more profound. Newspapers are losing readers and political parties are losing members. The old players of democracy are bobbing about amid the wreckage, clinging to each other, not realising that by doing so they are only dragging each other further down. Tied as it is to formats, circulation figures, shareholders and obligatory hotheadedness, the free press is far less free than it thinks and the outcome is inevitable.

The collective hysteria of commercial media, social media and political parties has made election fever permanent and has serious consequences for the workings of democracy. Efficiency suffers under the electoral calculus, legitimacy under the continual need to distinguish oneself, while time and again the electoral system ensures that the long term and the common interest lose out to the short term and party interests. Elections were once invented to make democracy possible, but in these circumstances they would seem to be a definite hindrance.

As if destined to rid the system once and for all of any hope of tranquillity, the financial crisis of 2008 and the economic and monetary crisis that followed it added fuel to the flames. Populism, technocracy and anti-parliamentarianism have made their appearance and although not yet at the level of the 1930s, similarities to the situation in the 1920s are becoming more and more striking.

*

If the Founding Fathers in the United States and the heroes of the French Revolution had known in what context their method would be forced to function 250 years later, they would no doubt have prescribed a different model. Imagine having to develop a system today that would express the will of the people. Would it really be a good idea to have them all queue up at polling stations every four or five years with a bit of card in their hands and go into a dark booth to put a mark, not next to ideas but next to names on a list, names of people about whom restless reporting had been going on for months in a commercial environment that profits from restlessness? Would we still have the nerve to call what is in fact a bizarre, archaic ritual 'a festival of democracy'?

Since we have reduced democracy to representative democracy and representative democracy to elections, a valuable system is now mired in deep difficulties. For the first time since the American and French revolutions, the next election has become more important than the last election, an astonishing transformation. An election gives only a very provisional mandate these days, and making the best of the system we have is becoming increasingly difficult, as democracy is brittle, more so than at any time since the Second World War. If we don't watch out, it will gradually become a dictatorship of elections.

This process should not really surprise us. How many inventions of the late eighteenth century are still of much use in the present day – the stage coach, the air balloon, the snuffbox? It may not be a popular conclusion but it must be understood that nowadays elections are primitive and a democracy that reduces itself to elections is in mortal decline. It is indeed rather as if we were to limit air travel to the hot-air balloon, even though there are now high-tension cables, private planes, new climatic patterns, tornadoes and space stations.

New platforms are creating a new world and now the key question is, who will command the stage? Until the invention of printing, just a few hundred individuals – abbots, princes, kings – decided which texts were to be copied and which not, but the arrival of printing meant that suddenly thousands of people had that power. The old order was brought down by it and Gutenberg's invention facilitated the transition from the Middle Ages to the Renaissance. With the arrival of social media it seems as if everyone has a printing press today, even as if everyone has a scriptorium at his or her disposal. The citizen is no longer a reader but an editor-in-chief, and this has caused a profound power shift which means large, established companies can be brought to their knees by the actions of a few dissatisfied customers.[52] Apparently unshakeable dictatorships lose their grip on their populations once people organise themselves through social media. Political parties no longer bring voters together but are torn apart by them, as their classic patriarchal model of representation no longer works at a time when citizens have more of a say than ever before.

Representative democracy is in essence a vertical model, but the twenty-first century is increasingly horizontal. Dutch professor of transition management Jan Rotmans said recently: 'We go from centralised to decentralised, from vertical to horizontal, from top-down to bottom-up. It has taken us more than a hundred years to build this centralised, top-down, vertical society. That whole way of thinking is now being turned upside down. There is a great deal we need to learn and unlearn. The greatest barrier is in our heads.'[53]

Elections are the fossil fuel of politics. Whereas once they gave democracy a huge boost, much like the boost that oil gave the economy, it now it turns out they cause colossal problems of their own. If we don't urgently reconsider the nature of our democratic fuel, a huge systemic crisis threatens. If we obstinately continue to hold on to the electoral process at a time of economic malaise, inflammatory media and rapidly changing culture, we will be almost wilfully undermining the democratic process.

How did we reach this point?

III

Pathogenesis

A democratic procedure: Drawing lots (antiquity and Renaissance)

Professor Verdin was one of the most captivating professors I've ever known. In my first year at university he taught me Historical Method, a dry but necessary subject, and the History of Greece. In those weekly lectures Verdin, in a genial voice, revealed Minoan civilisation to us, along with the government of Sparta, the growth of the Athenian fleet and the conquests of Alexander the Great. He was a professor of the old-fashioned kind, having no use for slides and transparencies, and PowerPoint had yet to be invented. Wearing a suit and tie, naturally, with heavy spectacles and snow-white hair, he simply told a great story for two hours. Verdin was erudite, eloquent and humane. It was the autumn of 1989 and I'd just begun my degree in archaeology.

One Monday morning, shortly before the lecture began, one of my fellow students held out his hands to show us some crumbling lumps of stone. He'd been to Berlin at the weekend for a good time. The Wall had fallen a few days before and as a future archaeologist, he'd pocketed some chunks of concrete in the middle of a drunken night.

Verdin – he didn't have a first name – told us about the institutions of fifth-century Athens, the century of Pericles, the Greek city state and the birth of democracy. We believed we were now about to hear details of the glorious tradition in which the East Germans, too, were soon to take part.

But the world evoked by the professor was miles away from what we'd been following live on television. I still have my notes. 'Goal: political equality,' I read in the handwriting that was once mine, and underneath: 'purely of the citizens, not the entire population: small minority, therefore'. I remember feeling a slight disappointment. All of Berlin had stood in the cold, swaying and chanting *Wir sind das Volk*, but in ancient Athens hardly any of those people in parkas would have been allowed to participate. 'In using the term "democratisation",' Verdin's programme of lectures made clear, 'we must of course not lose sight of an essential feature of the polis, namely the exclusive nature of civil rights.' Women, foreigners, minors and slaves didn't count.

But it was stranger even than that. The three most important organs were the Public Assembly, the Council of 500 and the People's Court. Any citizen could take part, but there were three aspects to which we needed to 'give due account', as he solemnly put it.

'First, the participation of citizens was direct, in contrast to our current system in which representatives of the people are specialists to a far greater degree. Today only a jury in a criminal case is truly made up of ordinary citizens. Second, important decisions were taken by very large crowds in the Ekklesia or People's Assembly, where thousands came together. The Heliaia or People's Court had six thousand members and some juries consisted of hundreds of citizens. This too is at odds with our system, in which there is a certain oligarchisation of democracy.'

'Oligarchisation': typical Verdin, but the most remarkable fact of all was yet to come. 'Third, most functions were assigned by drawing lots, including to a large extent that of magistrate.' This made me sit up and pay attention. I'd just reached the voting age of eighteen and soon I'd be able to choose for the first time a person or persons and a party that seemed the most trustworthy to me. On paper it sounded great, that Athenian concept of equality, but did I want to live in the kind of tombola democracy about which Verdin was now giving us further details? And perhaps more importantly, was that what all those East Germans wanted, who were now going out onto the streets to demand free elections?

'This drawing of lots, or sortition, had its advantages,' Verdin continued calmly, 'as the aim was to neutralise personal influence. In Rome there was no such system and countless corruption scandals were the result. Moreover, in Athens posts were for just one year and generally speaking people were not eligible for re-election. At all levels, citizens were made to switch places as often as possible, the aim being to achieve maximum participation and therefore equality. Sortition and rotation were right at the heart of the Athenian democratic system.'

I wavered between enthusiasm and scepticism. Could I have had any faith in a governing team that was not elected but chosen by lot? How on earth was that supposed to work? How could you avoid blunders?

'The Athenian system was pragmatic rather than dogmatic,' Verdin told us, 'and it arose not from a theory but from experience. Sortition was not used for top military and financial functions; instead elections took place, and as rotation was not compulsory competent figures could be re-elected. Pericles, to take one example, was chosen as a *strategos* fourteen years in a row. The principle of equality was thereby subordinated to the principle of security. But this applied to only a minority of governmental mandates.'

I left the auditorium sadder but wiser. The mythical crucible of our democracy had turned out to be an archaic system with ramshackle procedures. Sortition and rotation were no doubt perfectly suitable for small city states of long ago, when men in sandals with sheets over their shoulders were able to chat for hours on sandy market squares about the construction of a new temple or a well. But as inspiration for the turbulent present? The crumbled concrete of the Berlin Wall continued to burn in our restless hands.

Not long ago I retrieved Professor Verdin's course from my archives (I've since learned that his name was Herman). If our Democratic Fatigue Syndrome is indeed caused by today's electoral-representative democracy, if our crisis of democracy is the fault of the specific procedure to which we limit it, if elections increasingly restrict democracy rather than advance it, then perhaps it might be useful to look at how the desire for democracy was interpreted in the past.

I'm not the only one to be curious. Over recent years, interest in the history of our current system has grown in academic circles. Truly groundbreaking was a 1995 book by French political scientist Bernard Manin, called *The Principles of Representative Government*.[54] The opening sentence was a bombshell. 'Contemporary democratic governments have evolved from a political system that was conceived by its founders as opposed to democracy.' Manin was the first to investigate the reason why elections are so important. His research revealed how, immediately after the American and French revolutions, the electoral-representative system was chosen with the intention of keeping at bay the tumult of democracy. 'Representative government was instituted in full awareness that elected representatives would and should be distinguished citizens, socially different from those who elected them.'

An aristocratic reflex lay at the basis of today's democracy and the extraordinarily far-reaching conclusion was that the representative system we know everywhere today 'includes both democratic and undemocratic features'.[55] I will return to this point.

In the wake of Manin's brilliant account, several innovative books have appeared over the past few years.[56] What these more recent studies demonstrate is that our current democracy is the result of a chance conjunction of circumstances over the past two hundred years, and they shine a refreshingly clear light on preceding centuries, revealing the existence of other possible forms of democracy.

So what was there before the American and French revolutions? In various places in antiquity and the Renaissance, the drawing of lots was relied upon.

In classical Athens of the fifth and fourth centuries BC, to return to those times for a moment, the most important organs of government were indeed manned by means of sortition, the Council of 500 (Boule), the People's Court (Heliaia) and practically all the magistracies (arkhai). The Council of 500 was the central governmental body of Athenian democracy: it prepared the agenda of the People's Assembly (Ekklesia), it oversaw finances, public works and the magistracies and it was even responsible for diplomatic relations with neighbouring powers. Citizens chosen by lot were at the nerve centre of power, and of the seven hundred magistrates, six hundred were appointed by sortition while the rest were elected. The People's Court chose hundreds of jury members almost every morning by lot, out of a pool of six thousand citizens. Each tribe used a *kleroterion*, a large standing stone with five columns of slots into which aspiring jury members put their nameplates. Coloured balls were pulled out of a locked vertical cylinder next to the stone, each of which corresponded with one of the nameplates on the *kleroterion*. Those whose names were drawn got the job. It was gambling for the prize of being allowed to administer justice, a kind of roulette designed to distribute power fairly.

Sortition was used to allocate legislative, executive and judicial power (Figure 2B). Each new law was prepared by the Council of 500 and voted on by the People's Assembly, while the People's Court studied its legality and the magistrates took care of its implementation. The Council of 500 controlled the executive, while the People's Court fulfilled the role of the judiciary.

One striking thing about Athenian democracy was the rapid switching of mandates. You were a judge for one day, a councillor or magistrate – a paid position – for one year. You could not sit on the council for more than two non-consecutive terms. Anyone who felt capable of filling a governmental post could put themselves forward as a candidate, leading to broad participation. In fact 50 to 70% of citizens over the age of thirty had once sat on the Council.

FIGURES 2A + 2B: The most important organs of Athenian democracy (fifth and fourth centuries BC) and the distribution of legislative, executive and judicial power

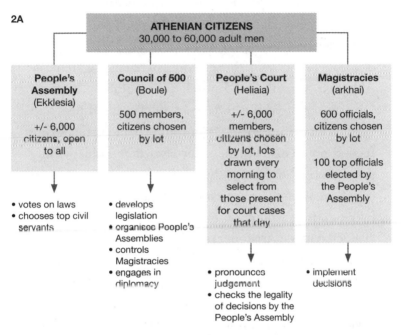

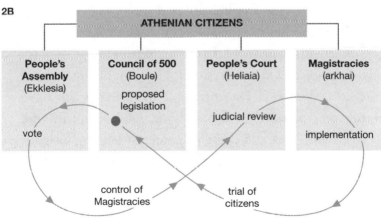

Nowadays we might perhaps be surprised that Athenian democracy, in its heyday, relied on something as unfamiliar to us as the drawing of lots, but for contemporaries it was simply self-evident that it should. Aristotle put it frankly: 'For example, the appointment of magistrates by lot is democratical, and the election of them oligarchical.' Although Aristotle was himself an advocate of a mixed form, he brought the difference between sortition and election into focus by calling the former democratic and the second not. This is made clear elsewhere in his writing too: he noted of Sparta that the constitution contained countless oligarchic elements and 'that all offices are filled by election and none by lot is one of these oligarchical characteristics'. Aristotle regarded the drawing of lots as truly democratic. Typical of Athenian democracy was the fact that virtually no distinction existed between politicians and citizens, between the governing and the governed or between holders of power and subjects. The function of 'career politician' that we all find so natural today would have seemed totally bizarre and absurd to the average Athenian, and Aristotle linked this to an extremely interesting idea about freedom. 'The basis of a democratic state is liberty ... One principle of liberty is for all to rule and be ruled in turn.'[57] Twenty-five centuries old, Aristotle's work still presents some astonishing insights. Freedom does not mean always having power yourself. Nor does it mean being free of the need to pay attention to power or slavishly reconciling yourself to power. Freedom means finding a balance between autonomy and loyalty, between ruling and being ruled. This is an insight that today, with the 'oligarchising of democracy' now far more rife than twenty-five years ago when Professor Verdin warned of it, seems to have been entirely forgotten.

Athenian democracy is often described as direct democracy. Verdin told us about the great monthly People's Assembly in which thousands of citizens took an active part. In the fourth century BC, it met almost weekly. But most of the work was done in other, more specific institutions such as the People's Court, the Council of 500 and the magistracies. There, not all the people spoke but instead a random sample, chosen by lot. The people of Athens did not all participate directly in the decisions taken by these bodies. I would therefore agree completely with a recent study that describes Athenian democracy not as a direct democracy but as a uniquely representative democracy, a non-electoral representative democracy.[58] Actually I would go a step further. Because representation of the people was brought about by the drawing of lots, we might speak of an aleatoric-representative democracy (from the Latin for dice). Aleatoric-representative democracies are indirect forms of government in which the distinction between ruler and ruled is brought about by sortition rather than election, and the political history of Western Europe features more such systems than is generally realised.

*

FIGURE 3: Sortition as a political instrument in antiquity and the Renaissance

	Athens *Kleroterion* (462-322 BC)	Venice *Ballotta* (1268-1797)
Goal	• promote political equality • allow as many citizens as possible to participate in government	• avoid conflict between noble families in making appointments to high office
For whom	30,000 to 60,000 citizens (= 10 to 24% of 250,000 to 300,000 residents)	600 to 1,600 council members (= 0.6 to 1.2% of 100,000 to 135,000 residents)
Sortition	In appointing the most important organs of government: - Council of 500 - People's Court (6,000) - Magistracies (600)	In appointments to the highest office: - forming electoral committees to select the doge
How	1. self-selection 2. sortition (with *kleroterion*) 3. appointment	1. Consiglio Grande 2. 10 phases of sortition and election, alternating 3. lots in the form of balls
Rotation	after 1 year (max. 2 mandates)	
Elections	In appointing to the highest office: - 10 army leaders (*strategoi*) - 90 top civil servants	Election and sortition go hand in hand in the appointment of the doge
Elsewhere	Also in Milete and Kos; also in Hellenistic and early-Roman Athens (322-31); also in Roman Republic (Comitia Tributa)	Also in Parma, Ivrea, Brescia, Bologna

| Florence
Imborsazione (1328-1530) | Aragon
Insaculación (1350-1715) |
|---|---|
| • avoid conflict between rival factions | • promote stability
• counter monopolies of power |
| 7,000 to 8,000 citizens
(= 7 to 9% of 90,000 residents) | citizens
(= 1 to 16% (for municipal posts) of residents) |
| In appointing the most important organs of government
- legislative Council
- government (Signoria)
- governmental commissioners | In appointing
- electoral committees (see Venice)
- local officials (see Florence)
- national members of parliament (Corts) |
| 1. recommendation by guild or family
2. cooptation
3. sortition
4. selection | 1. recommendation
2. cooptation
3. sortition |
rapid rotation, no cumulation	rapid rotation: 1 year
Cooptation as top-down election	Cooptation as top-down election
Also in Orvieto, Siena, Pistoia, Perugia, Lucca, even Münster and Frankfurt	Also in Zaragoza, Gerona, Tarragona, Huesca, Cervera, Ciutadella, Majorca, Lleida, Igualada; also in La Mancha, Murcia and Extramadura

In the Roman Republic, several traces were to be found of the Athenian system of selection by lot, but it fell into disuse in the imperial period. Only with the rise of the northern Italian city states in the Middle Ages did the procedure come back into vogue. In Bologna (1245), Vicenza (1264), Novara (1287) and Pisa (1307), we see early examples, but the great Renaissance cities of Venice (1268) and Florence (1328) are the best documented (Figure 3).

Both Venice and Florence worked with sortition, if in utterly different ways. In Venice it was used for centuries to appoint the head of state, the doge (a word equivalent to *duce*, 'duke'). The Venetian Republic was no democracy; it was an oligarchy run by several powerful aristocratic families, its government in the hands of a few hundred or a few thousand nobles, no more than 1% of the population. A quarter to a third of them filled practically all government posts and whoever became doge remained so until his death, although in contrast to a monarchy the position was not hereditary. To prevent tensions between the ruling families, sortition was introduced as a way of appointing a new doge, but in order to ensure only a competent person could become ruler, the procedure was combined with elections. The result was an unbelievably roundabout system that took place in ten phases over a period of five days. It started with the Grand Council (Consiglio Grande), on which five hundred nobles had seats (the number increased from the fourteenth century onwards). Every one of them placed a wooden ball (*ballotta*) with his name on it in an urn, while the youngest left the council chamber, went to St Mark's Basilica and approached a boy aged between eight and ten at random. He was asked to join the conclave and given the role of *ballottino*. The innocent child's hand drew the names of thirty participants which were then whittled down to nine in a further round. These men formed the first election committee and their task was to expand the group of nine again to forty, by a system of qualified majority voting (in reality this was a kind of co-option). Those forty were then reduced to twelve by lot, and those twelve were able to vote until there were twenty-five. It went on like this for a while, the electoral commission repeatedly reducing by lot and then expanding by vote, using the aleatoric and electoral methods by turns. The ninth and penultimate round produced an electoral commission with forty-one names who then came together to choose the doge.

The Venetian system seems absurdly cumbersome, but recently several computer scientists have shown that this leader election protocol is interesting in that it ensured the more popular candidates actually won, while nevertheless giving minorities a chance and neutralising corrupt voting behaviour. Furthermore, it helped to bring compromise candidates to the fore by amplifying small advantages.[59] All this benefitted both the legitimacy and the efficiency of the newly appointed leader. In any case, historians agree that the extraordinary lasting stability of the Venetian Republic, which endured for more than five centuries until ended by Napoleon, can be attributed in part to the ingenious system of *ballotte*. Without sortition the republic would undoubtedly have fallen prey far sooner to disputes between ruling families. (You do quietly wonder whether today's governments are not similarly falling prey to the bickering between parties.)

A small historical point worth noting is that the memory of the Venetian system endured in its nomenclature alone. By one of those rare twists on which etymology has a patent, the English word 'ballot' is directly derived from the Italian *ballotte*, those balls used in the drawing of lots.

The system was different in Florence, where it was known as *imborsazione* (insertion). Here too the aim was to avoid conflict between interest groups in the city, but the people of Florence went far further than the Venetians. They decided to apportion not just the job of head of state but practically all administrative tasks and governmental responsibilities by lot. If Venice was a republic of aristocratic families, Florence became a republic in which prominent citizens and powerful corporations called the shots. As in ancient Athens, the most important governmental institutions were staffed by citizens chosen by lot: the government (Signoria), the legislative council and the commissioners. The Signoria, like the Council of 500 in Athens, was the highest executive institution, responsible for foreign policy, administrative control and even the preparation of legislation. In contrast to Athens, citizens could not put their own names forward but had to be nominated by their guild, their family or some other organisation, after which they were called *nominati.* A second selection procedure then took place when a commission made up of a diverse range of residents decided by vote who would be considered for jobs in government. Only then did *la tratta,* the drawing of lots, take place, after some names were eliminated such as those of people who already occupied positions of authority or who had been convicted of crimes. The process therefore took place in four stages: nomination, election, sortition, deletion. As in Athens, any accumulation of functions was forbidden and those appointed had to leave office after a year. Also as in Athens, the system ensured the involvement of ordinary citizens, as no fewer than 75% of them were nominated. *Nominati* had no idea whether or not they would get through the second phase as that list remained secret, so if you were not appointed to one of a couple of thousand government jobs, it might be because of the drawing of lots or because of the way the voting had gone.

While the Venetian model was adopted in cities including Parma, Ivrea, Brescia and Bologna, the Florentine system was applied in Orvieto, Siena, Pistoia, Perugia and Lucca. Countless lucrative trading contacts took it as far as Frankfurt am Main. On the Iberian Peninsula several cities in the Kingdom of

Aragon adopted the procedure, including Lleida (1386), Zaragoza (1443), Gerona (1457) and Barcelona (1498). There sortition became known as *la insaculación*, literally 'drawing lots out of a sack', a term derived from the Spanish translation of the Italian *imborsazione*. The aim once again was to promote stability by means of a neutral distribution of governmental power. The issue of who was allowed to occupy a position of authority in the city or region or to take a seat on the electoral commission was no longer the subject of an endless tug of war. The decision was made quickly and even-handedly. The dissatisfied could comfort themselves with the thought that they would soon have another chance. As in Athens and Florence, a post filled by lot could not be occupied for more than a year. This rapid rotation naturally encouraged participation, and in Spain's other great kingdom, Castile, sortition was used in regions including Murcia, La Mancha and Extremadura. When in 1492 Ferdinand II added the Kingdom of Castile to his Kingdom of Aragon, thus laying the foundation for present-day Spain, he said, 'Experience shows that cities and municipalities that work with sortition are more likely to promote the good life, a healthy administration and a sound government than regimes based on elections. They are more harmonious and egalitarian, more peaceful and disengaged with regard to the passions.'[60]

In retrospect, this fleeting overview of history teaches us six things. 1) Since antiquity, sortition has been used as a valuable political instrument in several states. 2) In all cases these were geographically small, urbanised states (the city state, the civic republic) where only a limited segment of the population could participate in government. 3) The use of lots often coincided with the peak period of prosperity and culture (Athens in the fourth and fifth centuries, Venice and Florence during the Renaissance). 4) There were various applications and procedures, but drawing lots generally resulted in less conflict and more participation by citizens. 5) Sortition was never deployed exclusively but always in combination with elections, in order to guarantee competence. 6) States that used sortition often experienced centuries of political stability, despite great internal differences between rival groups. The tiny state of San Marino drew lots as recently as the mid-twentieth century in order to choose two governors from its sixty-member governing council.[61]

In the eighteenth century, the century of the Enlightenment, great philosophers turned their attention to the democratic form of government. Montesquieu, founder of the modern constitutional state, repeated in his *The Spirit of the Laws* of 1748 the insight that Aristotle had expressed two millennia earlier, 'Voting by *lot* is in the nature of democracy; voting by *choice* is in the nature of aristocracy.' The elite character of elections was clear to him from the start. In contrast, he claimed, 'the casting of lots is a way of electing that distresses no one; it leaves to each citizen a reasonable expectation of serving his country.' That it was good for the citizen was obvious, but was it also good for the country? The danger of incompetent people coming to power through sortition had to be averted by means of selection, self-selection or evaluation. Montesquieu praised Athenian democracy because functionaries had to justify the way they conducted themselves. It meant there were elements both of election and of sortition.[62] Only by combining the two systems could problems be avoided – pure sortition led to incompetence, pure election led to impotence.

We find similar ideas in the famous *Encyclopaedia* compiled by Diderot and d'Alembert in the 1750s. In the entry headed 'aristocracy' we read that the drawing of lots was not suitable for the aristocracy ('Suffrage must not be given by lot; only inconveniences would result from it'). It was better to appoint a senate. 'In that case, one might say that aristocracy is in a way, in the senate, democracy in the body of nobles, and that the people are nothing.' The authors make it clear that the aristocracy has a responsibility for the people and in the entry for democracy they largely adopt Montesquieu's arguments.

A few years later, Rousseau developed their thinking further. He too found a mixed form attractive, especially when it came to allocating jobs: 'When the two forms of election, that by vote and that by lot, are mixed, the first should be used to fill places which require men of special talents, such as military offices; the other, when good sense, justice, and integrity are sufficient, as they are in judicial offices.' Rousseau described the combined method that ancient Athens used for centuries to make government appointments. The combination of sortition and election resulted in a system that enjoyed great legitimacy and at the same time could be efficient. Of course in every society, talents are unevenly distributed, but that does not mean sortition could be written off. 'If we consider that the election of chiefs is one of the functions of government, and not of sovereignty, we shall perceive why the mode of choosing them by lot is more natural to a democracy,' he wrote. 'In all true democracies the office of a magistrate is so far from being advantageous that it is a very burdensome charge, which cannot justly be imposed on one individual rather than on another. The law alone can impose the charge on the person upon whom the lot falls.'[63]

The conclusion is clear, and despite important differences between the authors, the two most important books about the political philosophy of the eighteenth century agree that sortition is more democratic than election and that a combination of the two methods is beneficial to society. The aleatoric and electoral procedures can mutually reinforce each other.

An aristocratic procedure: Elections (eighteenth century)

And then something strange happens. Bernard Manin describes it beautifully:

> Scarcely one generation after the *Spirit of the Laws* and the *Social Contract*, however, the idea of attributing public functions by lot had vanished almost without trace. Never was it seriously considered during the American and French revolutions. At the same time that the founding fathers were declaring the equality of all citizens, they decided without the slightest hesitation to establish, on both sides of the Atlantic, the unqualified dominion of a method of selection long deemed to be aristocratic.[64]

How could this be? How did it come about that the arguments of the most influential philosophers of the time were ignored, in a century that nonetheless continually made appeal to reason and to *les philosophes*? Where did this one-sided triumph of the aristocratic idea of elections come from? And how can it be that sortition, as we might put it today, completely disappeared from the radar?

For some time historians and political scientists were faced with a puzzle. Did it perhaps have to do with practical objections? Yes, there was definitely a difference in scale as drawing lots in ancient Athens, a city of a few square kilometres, was a rather different matter from doing so in a country the size of France or in the huge area covered by the thirteen newly independent states on the Atlantic coast of North America. Travelling time alone meant they were a totally different universe, and that was certainly part of the picture.

At the end of the eighteenth century, national population registers and demographic statistics were not yet sufficiently developed to give sortition a fair chance. No one knew how many inhabitants a country had, let alone how a representative sample could be taken. Moreover, a profound and detailed knowledge of Athenian democracy did not yet exist. The first thorough study, *Election by Lot at Athens* by James Wycliffe Headlam, was not published for another century, in 1891. Before that there were only a few incomplete insights, as described in occasional works such as *Of the Nature and Use of Lots: A Treatise Historicall and Theologicall* by the Reverend Thomas Gataker, published in 1627.

Practical objections cannot have been the only reason, however. The ancient Athenians didn't have a perfect administrative grasp of the population and the residents of Florence lacked detailed knowledge of what had happened in Greece, yet they both used sortition on a large scale. What stands out in the writings of American and French revolutionaries is not so much the fact that they couldn't apply the drawing of lots but that they didn't want to apply it; in fact at no time do they even seem to have been inclined to try. The reasons for this were not merely practical, as none complain that the drawing of lots might not have been feasible, but it becomes increasingly obvious that to them it was in any case undesirable, and this had to do with their beliefs about democracy.

For Montesquieu there were three distinct forms of government; monarchy, despotism and the republic. In a monarchy one person was in charge, according to the laws laid down. Despotism also meant the leadership of a single person but without any established laws, which made it arbitrary in the extreme. In a republic, power lay with the people, and with regard to this third form of government he made another extremely important distinction. 'When the people as a body have sovereign power, it is a democracy. When the sovereign power is in the hands of a part of the people, it is called an aristocracy.'[65]

We know well enough that the upper bourgeoisie, which threw off the British and French crowns in 1776 and 1789, fought for a republican form of government, but whether it was devoted to the democratic variety of that form of government is open to question. There are certainly plenty of references to 'the people', the revolutionaries repeatedly declaring that they believed the people were sovereign, that the Nation should be spelt with a capital 'N' and that 'We the People' was the start of everything. But when it came down to it they nevertheless had a fairly elitist concept of 'the people'. The newly independent states of North America were called 'republics' not 'democratic republics'. John Adams, the great campaigner for independence and second president of the United States, was extremely hesitant about the system and warned, 'Remember, democracy never lasts long. It soon wastes, exhausts, and murders itself. There never was a democracy yet that did not commit suicide.'[66] James Madison, father of the American constitution, was convinced that democracies had always been 'spectacles of turbulence and contention', which generally speaking 'have been as short in their lives as they have been violent in their deaths'.[67]

In revolutionary France, too, the term 'democracy' was little used and tended to have negative connotations referring to the unrest that would break out if the poor came to power. One important revolutionary patriot, Antoine Barnave, member of the first Assemblée Nationale, described *la démocratie* as 'the most hateful, the most subversive and for the people the most damaging of all political systems'.[68] In the French debates about suffrage held between 1789 and 1791, which gave rise to the constitution, the term democracy does not occur once.[69]

Canadian political scientist Francis Dupuis-Déri has investigated the use of the word 'democracy' and discovered that the fathers of the American and French revolutions clearly avoided using it, as most of them thought democracy represented chaos and extremism and they wanted nothing to do with either. But this was not merely a matter of the choice of words. The reality of democracy would naturally be an abomination to them, since many were lawyers, large landowners, factory owners, shipping magnates, and in America plantation owners and slave owners. They had often held posts in government and operated in political roles under the British or French crowns, when the era of aristocracy was in its prime, and they had social and family ties with the system they opposed.[70] 'This elite therefore strove to undermine the legitimacy of the king or the aristocracy. In one and the same movement they emphasised the political inability of the people to govern themselves. They also loudly announced that the nation was sovereign, and they, the elite, wanted to serve its interests.'[71]

In that context the term 'republic' sounded nobler than 'democracy' and elections became more important than drawing lots. The revolutionary leaders in France and the US had no desire for sortition because they had no desire for democracy. A person who has taken over a luxury coach from an ancient grandfather does not immediately allow the grandchildren to drive it.

To return to the typology of Montesquieu, while the patriotic leaders of the French and American revolutions were decidedly republican, it was in a far from democratic sense. They did not want to allow the people to drive the coach of power but preferred to keep hold of the reins, to prevent inevitable chaos. In the United States, the elite, whose economic privileges were considerable, had a great deal to lose by relinquishing power and in France this was no less true, but there was something else at play here. In contrast to the US, the new society had to be built on the same territory as that of the previous regime, so for the new elite it was important to find a compromise with the old landed nobility. In other words, sitting in the coach the revolutionaries took over were many ancient aristocrats, and anyone wanting to set off on a new course had to take some account of the travel advice of those obstinate passengers, if only because they might otherwise put a spoke in the wheels.

It soon became clear in both countries that the republic the revolutionary leaders had in mind, and to which they then gave shape, tended more to the aristocratic than the democratic. Elections could help.

Nowadays that conclusion might sound heretical. After all, how often have we heard that modern democracy begins with the revolutions of 1776 and 1789? A careful analysis of the historical texts, however, tells a very different story.[72]

In the year of independence, 1776, John Adams wrote in his famous *Thoughts on Government* that America was too big and too populous to be governed directly. That was simply a fact and indiscriminately transposing the model of Athens or Florence could never have worked. But the outcome of his reasoning was rather odd, as he argued that the most important step was 'to depute power from the many, to a few of the most wise and good'. If the people as a whole could not speak, a circle of the most outstanding must do so in their place. In a rather naive, utopian way, Adams hoped that a gathering of such virtuous people would 'think, feel, reason, and act' like the rest of society. 'It should be in miniature, an exact portrait of the people at large.' Of course the question was whether a banker from New York and a lawyer from Boston, if they sat down together, could feel the same sympathy for the needs and grievances of a baker's wife in a settlement in Massachusetts or a dockworker in New Jersey as they did for each other's needs and grievances.

Ten years later, James Madison looked into this in more depth. The Articles of Confederation of 1777 were to be replaced by a proper constitution for a federal America, and Madison, who wrote the initial version, moved heaven and earth to have his draft ratified in the thirteen states of the then confederation. In the 'Federalist Papers', a series of eighty-five essays that he and two colleagues published in New York newspapers in their efforts to persuade the state of New York to ratify, he wrote in February 1788:

The aim of every political Constitution is or ought to be first to obtain for rulers, men who possess most wisdom to discern, and most virtue to pursue the common good of the society; and in the next place, to take the most effectual precautions for keeping them virtuous . . . The elective mode of obtaining rulers is the characteristic policy of republican government.[73]

With that preference for men who possess most wisdom to discern, and most virtue to pursue the common good of society, Madison connects seamlessly with John Adams but it also puts him miles away from the Athenian ideal of the equal distribution of political opportunities. Whereas to the Greek mind as little distinction as possible was to be made between governors and the governed, for Madison such a distinction was desirable. Whereas Aristotle thought it a sign of freedom to govern and be governed by turns, for the American father of the constitution it was better if the most wise and virtuous kept the reins firmly in their own hands.[74]

A government led by the best – did that not mean *aristokratia* in Greek? Thomas Jefferson, the father of American independence, believed there was such a thing as 'a natural aristocracy among men' and he went on to say that 'the grounds for this are virtue and talents'. He said that the best form of government 'provides the most effectively for a pure selection of these natural *aristoi* into the offices of government'.[75]

He did not believe that this would lead to 'a pretended oligarchy', because the best would come to power through elections, and furthermore, it was not only more efficient to work with them, but because of the electoral procedure it was also legitimate. His reasoning was as follows:

> Who are to be the electors of the Federal Representatives? Not the rich more than the poor; not the learned more than the ignorant; not the haughty heirs of distinguished names, more than the humble sons of obscure and unpropitious fortune. The electors are to be the great body of the people of the United States.

He does not mention the fact that women, 'Indians', black people, the poor and slaves were not to be counted among them, nor was it an obstacle that he himself was the owner of large slave plantations in Virginia. While it is also true that only a small number of the elite could hope for a share of power in ancient Greece, in this case what was different was that in the electoral-representative system Madison proposed, in contrast to the system of drawing lots, those in government would be distinguished qualitatively from those they governed. He even says so in so many words:

Who are to be the objects of popular choice? Every citizen whose merit may recommend him to the esteem and confidence of his country . . . As they will have been distinguished by the preference of their fellow citizens, we are to presume, that in general, they will be somewhat distinguished also, by those qualities which entitle them to it.

It would therefore be necessary to have merits, to inspire esteem and confidence, to be different, better, superlative. The representative system may have been democratic in that it gave people the vote, but it was aristocratic from the start in its form of recruitment. Anyone could vote, but a selection had already been made that favoured the elite.

There, at that spot, is where in practice it began, with those words of James Madison, in 'Federalist Paper' number 57, published on 19 February 1788 in the newspaper *The New York Packet*. Or rather, that is where it ended, where the idea of Athenian democracy – equal distribution of political opportunities – was buried. From then on there must at all costs be a distinction between competent governors and the incompetent governed. This looks more like the start of a technocracy than of a democracy.

*

87

In French documents too, the aristocratisation of the revolution is visible. The tumult started with a popular revolt, which was tempered after a while by a new, bourgeois elite that wanted to 'put affairs in order', in other words to govern the land and safeguard its own interests. In the US this process took place between independence in 1776 and the constitution of 1789 (with Madison in the leading role), in France between the uproar of 1789 and the constitution of 1791. The revolt in which the ordinary people had participated (including the storming of the Bastille, which assumed mythical proportions) would within a few years result in a constitution according to which participation was limited to the right to vote and that right was given to no more than one in six Frenchmen.

The *Declaration of the Rights of Man and of the Citizen*, the most important document of the 1789 revolution, stated: 'The law is the expression of the general will. All citizens have the right to contribute personally, or through their representatives, to its formation.' But in the constitution of 1791, that personal involvement has gone completely: 'The nation, from which alone all powers emanate, may exercise such powers only by delegation. The French Constitution is representative.' Within three years, the power to initiate legislation had shifted from the people to the representatives of the people, so the system was no longer participative but representative.

Particularly striking is the attitude of Abbé Sieyès, a Catholic priest from Fréjus, whose pamphlet *What is the Third Estate?* lit the revolutionary touch paper. Sieyès, the man who believed that the aristocracy and the clergy, the first and second estates, had far too much power compared to the third estate, the citizenry, the man who appealed for more citizen participation and the abolition of aristocratic privileges, the man whose work was read by everyone (more than thirty thousand copies of his pamphlet were sold in January 1789), the man who gave frustration a voice and was regarded as one of the most important theoreticians of the revolution, even he believed France was not a democracy and must not become one. He wrote: 'In a country that is not a democracy – and France cannot be one – the people, I repeat, can speak or act only through its representatives.'[76]

Since then there has existed something we might call 'political agoraphobia', a fear of the man in the street – even among revolutionaries.[77] Once the parliament has been chosen, the people must hold their tongues. The drawing of lots has been confined to one specific domain of public life: the selection of juries for certain criminal trials.

The aristocratisation of the revolution must have given Edmund Burke a great deal of pleasure. The British philosopher and politician was seriously disturbed, not to say frightened, by the idea that the people would be given too much power. In his elegantly written *Reflections on the Revolution in France* (1790) he notes that rulers must distinguish themselves from the rest, not by 'blood and names and titles' – he too was aware that times were changing – but through 'virtue and wisdom'. And he added:

> The occupation of a hairdresser or of a working tallow-chandler cannot be a matter of honour to any person – to say nothing of a number of other more servile employments. Such descriptions of men ought not to suffer oppression from the state; but the state suffers oppression if such as they, either individually or collectively, are permitted to rule . . . Everything ought to be open, but not indifferently, to every man. No rotation; no appointment by lot; no mode of election operating in the spirit of sortition or rotation can be generally good in a government conversant in extensive objects.

Goodbye to the Athenian ideal. It's the most explicit eighteenth-century rejection of sortition of which I am aware. Burke was against democracy, against Rousseau, against the revolution and against sortition. He preferred to praise the competence of the elite: 'I do not hesitate to say that the road to eminence and power, from obscure condition, ought not to be made too easy, nor a thing too much of course . . . The temple of honour ought to be seated on an eminence.'[78]

Burke's words did not fall on deaf ears. During negotiations on the new French constitution of 1795 after the turbulent years of the Terror, the chairman of the convention, Boissy D'Anglas, who was required to prepare the text, spoke as follows:

> We should be governed by the best; the best are the best educated and the most interested in the maintenance of the laws: apart from a few exceptions, you will not find such men except among those who, possessing property, are attached to the land that contains it, to the laws that protect it, to the tranquillity that preserves it . . . A country governed by property holders is in the social order; that in which the non-property holders govern is in the state of nature.[79]

The French Revolution, like the American, did not dislodge the aristocracy to replace it with a democracy but rather dislodged a hereditary aristocracy to replace it with an elected aristocracy, '*une aristocratie élective*', to use Rousseau's term. Robespierre even called it '*une aristocratie représentative*'.[80] The prince and the noble were sent packing, the people were fobbed off with rhetoric about *la Nation*, *le Peuple* and *la Souveraineté*, and a new upper bourgeoisie took power. It derived its legitimacy no longer from God, soil or birth but from another relic of the aristocratic era, elections. This explains the exhausting arguments about suffrage and the severe limitations placed on it, as only those who paid sufficient tax could qualify. Only one out of every six citizens of France was allowed to vote in the first parliamentary elections, according to the constitution of 1791. The fiery revolutionary Jean-Paul Marat denounced the aristocratisation of the popular revolt and took up the cause of the more than eighteen million French people who were not given a vote. 'What use is it to us,' he wrote, 'that we have broken the aristocracy of the nobles, if that is replaced by the aristocracy of the rich?'

The democratisation of elections: A bogus process (nineteenth and twentieth centuries)

To recapitulate for a moment. I ended Chapter II with the thought that elections are outdated as a democratic instrument, but we now learn something far worse, that they were never actually intended as a democratic instrument in the first place. Furthermore, the most commonly used democratic instrument, the drawing of lots, was completely rejected by the architects of the representative system with the exception of one limited domain, that of trial by jury. Electoral fundamentalists, we have for decades clung to the ballot box as if it were the Holy Grail of democracy, only to discover that we have been clinging not to a Holy Grail but to a poisoned chalice that was deliberately set up as an anti-democratic instrument.

How can it be that we failed for so long to see this? In order to fathom the pathogenesis of our electoral fundamentalism we need to take another step. The first step was to look at the physiology of aleatoric-representative democracy in antiquity and in the Renaissance. The second step was to recognise how in the late eighteenth century, a new elite pushed that tradition aside in favour of the electoral-representative system. What we now need to discover is how this system was able to retain democratic legitimacy in the nineteenth and twentieth centuries, until in recent years it came under fire. In other words, having examined the aristocratisation of the revolution we now need to look at the democratisation of elections.

The first thing to note is that the terminology changed and a republic based on suffrage, however limited, was increasingly referred to as a democracy. As early as 1851 an observer was able to determine that 'the elective aristocracy of which Rousseau spoke fifty years ago is what we now call representative democracy'.[81] This synonymy has since been completely forgotten, as nowadays hardly anyone is aware of the democratic roots of our current system.

When in the early nineteenth century Alexis de Tocqueville travelled through the United States for nine months in order to study the new form of government there, he had no hesitation in giving the book he wrote about his experiences the title *Democracy in America*. The reason for this is stated in the first sentence: 'Amongst the novel objects that attracted my attention during my stay in the United States, nothing struck me more forcibly than the general equality of conditions.' Nowhere else did a country exist, he believed, where the doctrine of the sovereignty of the people was considered to be of such paramount importance. His book was so extraordinarily influential in the nineteenth century that there can be little doubt it contributed to the growing popularity of the term 'democracy' as a description of the republican, electoral-representative system.

Note that this does not mean Tocqueville welcomed elections uncritically. He was an exceptional observer and, as a descendant of an old aristocratic family that had seen several of its members end their lives at the guillotine, he had every reason to regard the new system with the greatest suspicion. Nevertheless he displayed a passionate interest in, and openness to, what was happening in America. Unlike many aristocrats, he realised that the revolutions in the United States and in France had not been accidental occurrences but part of a far larger, centuries-long development towards greater equality. The trend could not be stopped, and for that reason he deliberately distanced himself from the old world. He never used his aristocratic title, left the Church and married a commoner. When in the 1830s he entered French politics himself, he lamented the fact that the system he had to work within was insufficiently democratic and offered citizens few opportunities for political participation.

His trip around America made Tocqueville a passionate democrat, but he remained critical of the actual forms the new system took. In both the United States and France, election had won out over sortition and lots were drawn only to put together a jury for certain types of court case.

In order to understand his attitude to these two methods of selection, it is worth citing his delightful prose at length. It's hard to believe that this passage about the electoral system was written as long ago as 1830:

> The wheels of government cease to act, as it were, of their own accord at the approach of an election, and even for some time previous to that event . . . At the approach of an election the head of the executive government is wholly occupied by the coming struggle; his future plans are doubtful; he can undertake nothing new, and he will only prosecute with indifference those designs which another will perhaps terminate . . . The eyes of the nation are centred on a single point; all are watching the gradual birth of so important an event . . . The period which immediately precedes an election and the moment of its duration must

always be considered as a national crisis . . . For a long while before the appointed time is at hand the election becomes the most important and the all-engrossing topic of discussion. The ardour of faction is redoubled; and all the artificial passions which the imagination can create in the bosom of a happy and peaceful land are agitated and brought to light. The President, on the other hand, is absorbed by the cares of self-defence. He no longer governs for the interest of the State, but for that of his re-election; he does homage to the majority, and instead of checking its passions, as his duty commands him to do, he frequently courts its worst caprices. As the election draws near, the activity of intrigue and the agitation of the populace increase; the citizens are divided into hostile camps, each of which assumes the name of its favourite candidate; the whole nation glows with feverish excitement; the election is the daily theme of the public papers, the subject of private conversation, the end of every thought and every action, the sole interest of the present. As soon as the choice is determined, this ardour is dispelled; and as a calmer season returns, the current of the State, which had nearly broken its banks, sinks to its usual level: but who can refrain from astonishment at the causes of the storm.[82]

This must be one of the earliest critiques of electoral-representative democracy, with its election fever, governmental paralysis, media frenzy, in short, its hysteria. Tocqueville is far more positive about the jury of one's peers, compiled by the drawing of lots, 'a certain number of citizens chosen indiscriminately, and invested with a temporary right of judging'. Here too it is worth quoting him at length:

> The jury, and more especially the jury in civil cases, serves to communicate the spirit of the judges to the minds of all the citizens; and this spirit, with the habits which attend it, is the soundest preparation for free institutions.

(Note how Tocqueville, just like Aristotle, makes a connection between freedom and the taking of responsibility on certain occasions, and how he describes freedom as something that people need to learn.)

> By obliging men to turn their attention to affairs which are not exclusively their own, it rubs off that individual egotism which is the rust of society. The jury contributes most powerfully to form the judgement and to increase the natural intelligence of a people, and this is, in my opinion, its greatest advantage. It may be regarded as a gratuitous public school ever open, in which every juror

learns to exercise his rights, enters into daily communication with the most learned and enlightened members of the upper classes, and becomes practically acquainted with the laws of his country, which are brought within the reach of his capacity by the efforts of the bar, the advice of the judge, and even by the passions of the parties. I think that the practical intelligence and political good sense of the Americans are mainly attributable to the long use which they have made of the jury in civil causes. I do not know whether the jury is useful to those who are in litigation; but I am certain it is highly beneficial to those who decide the litigation; and I look upon it as one of the most efficacious means for the education of the people which society can employ.[83]

Although at its beginnings American politics showed what a democracy was capable of, Tocqueville regretted the necessary evil of the electoral contest, even at a time when there were not yet any mass parties or mass media.

The years in which the two volumes of *Democracy in America* were published would be remembered for another event that helped to promote the electoral-representative system: the independence of Belgium in 1830. We might be surprised to learn that the emergence of a tiny country that had previously been ruled by foreign powers – since the French Revolution alone it had been in the possession of Austria, France and the Netherlands – could have such an impact. Yet that was the case. The constitution drawn up by the Belgians has gone down in history as the blueprint for the electoral-representative model.[84]

Belgian independence followed a familiar course of events. Following on from scuffles arising from opposition to the prevailing regime (August–September 1830), an aristocratisation of the revolution took place during the constitutional conference (November 1830–February 1831). The revolution had been the work of radicals, republicans and democrats but the constitution became a matter for aristocrats, clerics and moderate liberals. How could it be otherwise? This was 3 November 1830 and in elections to the National Congress, the first parliament, which was to write the constitution, only 46,000 men had the vote, less than 1% of the total population, because only those who paid sufficient tax could make their voices heard. The men responsible for determining the future of their country were mainly large landowners, aristocrats and members of the liberal professions, supplemented by a few 'capacitaire' voters, citizens who did not meet the fiscal threshold but were welcomed on the strength of their capacities, such as priests and university professors. The National Congress had two hundred members, forty-five of whom were aristocrats, thirty-eight lawyers, twenty-one magistrates and thirteen clergy. Half of them had held posts in public life before independence, so the break with the past was far less great than had been hoped.[85]

The revolutionary fervour was ended, the constitution became a moderate compromise with which other countries could live and upon which the nation could nourish itself. The conservative forces in society could satisfy themselves with three important elements: there would be a monarchy (not a republic), the fiscal threshold was maintained (rather than any expansion of suffrage) and there would be a senate (not simply a parliament). The latter point was particularly important, since it meant the aristocracy had an organ of its own in the new state, and because of the fiscal threshold, only a few of the very richest could aspire to a senate seat. A mere four hundred Belgians were eligible to be elected.

The progressive forces in young Belgian society managed to pull the following out of the fire: the power of the king was subordinated to that of the constitution and the parliament (there was talk of a constitutional or parliamentary monarchy), direct elections rather than indirect elections were held (in contrast to France and the US), press freedom and freedom of association were anchored in the constitution and jury members were to be selected by lot. The fiscal threshold for suffrage remained in force, but it was less restrictive than elsewhere. In Belgium one in every ninety-five citizens was given the vote whereas in France – where the monarchy had been restored by this point – the figure was one in 160.[86] Only the most radical elements involved in the popular revolt were left with empty hands.

Although three-quarters of the articles in the Belgian constitution were adopted from earlier constitutional texts deriving from France and the Netherlands, its originality lay in its sophisticated system of checks and balances between the various powers: head of state, parliament and government. Those qualities did not go unnoticed.

Nowadays few people are aware of the powerful influence exerted by that one text, but in the nineteenth century it was truly a reference point in the development of modern nation states. The constitution of Saxony (1831), the Swiss Confederation (1848) and the draft constitution for a federal Germany compiled by the Frankfurt Parliament (1849) adopted parts of it, and other constitutions were profoundly influenced by it, including that of Spain (1837). After the year of revolution, 1848, there was much imitation of it by those who put together constitutions in Greece (1848 and 1864), the Netherlands (1848), Luxembourg (1848), Piedmont Sardinia (1848), Prussia (1850), Romania (1866), Bulgaria (1879) and even the Ottoman Empire (1876). Those of the Netherlands, Luxembourg, Greece, Romania and Bulgaria in particular were faithful copies of the Belgian original. At the start of the twentieth century its influence extended even to Iran (1906) and in 1908 to the Ottoman Empire after the Young Turk Revolution in what was to become Turkey.

New Central European states such as Poland, Hungary and Czechoslovakia also drew upon it.[87]

A recent comparative study claims that 'The Belgian constitution of 1831 is among the most central constitutions produced prior to 1848'.[88] *The New Cambridge Modern History* speaks of a 'beacon', of a text that 'completely out-bid . . . practically every other European constitution of its day':

> This paragon of a constitution . . . contained so many features that were either unique or very much better than anything to be found elsewhere . . . that it is only to be wondered at that it was not more extensively copied than it was.[89]

In other words, a concise text of 139 articles would, for a century, decisively determine the constitutional form of large parts of the modern world. The electoral-representative model thereby became the norm, with Tocqueville giving that model the name 'democracy' and the Belgian constitution offering a blueprint for international use. From 1850 onwards, fighting for more democracy did not mean fighting against elections but fighting to extend suffrage, and the workers' movement on the rise all over Europe even made that one of its main points of contention. There was simply no demand for sortition, in fact the drawing of lots had acquired unpleasant connotations as it smacked of the hated system by which the army selected young recruits. The French had invented that system in the late eighteenth century and in Belgium, as elsewhere, the practice continued for another century, to the despair of many. In 1850, Hendrik Conscience, father of Flemish literature, made it the subject of his best work, in the novella *De loteling*.[90] Military drawing of lots had nothing to do with the equitable sharing out of political opportunities, of course. It purported, on paper at least, to be a way of distributing unpopular duties in a neutral fashion. In practice social inequality remained because rich young men who drew the short straw had plenty of money to pay a farm boy or worker's son to serve their time in the army for them. Working as it did to the advantage of the aristocracy, the aversion to drawing lots became deeply rooted in the lower classes and this represented a major historical reversal. Elections were suddenly regarded as democratic and sortition as aristocratic. No socialist foreman would ever appeal for sortition to be used politically and no village clergyman would ever defend it. Drawing lots was out.

When in 1891 the first major standard work about sortition in ancient Athens appeared, its author, James Wycliffe Headlam, who carried out his research at King's College, Cambridge, could hardly do otherwise than to open with the words: 'There is no institution of ancient history which is so difficult of comprehension as that of electing officials by the lot. We have ourselves no experience of the working of such a system; any proposal to introduce it now would appear so ludicrous that it requires some effort for us to believe that it ever did prevail in a civilised community.'[91]

Half a century later, in 1948, the Universal Declaration of Human Rights stated that 'The will of the people shall be the basis of the authority of government; this will shall be expressed in periodic and genuine elections'. Another half-century later, Francis Fukuyama announced 'the end of history' in a worldwide bestseller that celebrated a mystical marriage between parliamentary democracy and the free-market economy: 'A country is democratic if it grants its people the right to choose their own government through periodic, secret-ballot, multi-party elections, on the basis of universal and equal adult suffrage.'[92]

Voilà. Consensus complete.

Behold the pathogenesis of our electoral fundamentalism. The drawing of lots, the most democratic of all political instruments, lost out in the eighteenth century to elections, a procedure that was not invented as a democratic instrument but as a means of bringing a new, non-hereditary aristocracy to power. The extension of suffrage made that aristocratic procedure thoroughly democratic without relinquishing the fundamental, oligarchic distinction between governors and governed, between politicians and voters. Contrary to what Abraham Lincoln had hoped, the electoral democracy remained more 'government for the people' than 'government by the people'. There was something unavoidably vertical about it, always above and below, always a government and its subjects. Voting became the service lift that brought a few to the top, retaining therefore something of an elective feudalism, a form of internal colonialism that everyone endorsed.

The Democratic Fatigue Syndrome that is now emerging everywhere is a perfectly understandable consequence of the beatification of the electoral-representative system. For decades elections have kept the engine of democracy turning quite effectively, but now it's becoming increasingly obvious that they are a phenomenon borrowed from elsewhere. Yes, they have been polished vigorously in the past to make them fit more or less into the machinery of popular sovereignty, but after two centuries it is becoming clear that wear and tear is starting to have an effect. Efficiency sputters, legitimacy creaks and everywhere dissatisfaction, suspicion and protest are on the rise. Hardly surprising then that people are beginning to wonder if it is possible to imagine some other form of democracy, hardly surprising that in this context the idea of sortition is coming to the fore again.

IV

Remedies

There is an excellent saying often attributed to Gandhi, although in fact it comes from Central Africa: 'Whatever you do for me but without me, you do to me,' words that succinctly sum up the tragedy of today's electoral-representative democracy. Even with the best of intentions, those who govern the people without involving them, govern them in only a limited sense. In the eighteenth century, much of the population was illiterate and large areas of any country inaccessible, practical facts which had to be taken into consideration when the decision was made to hold elections. But is that still the case today?

The revival of sortition: Deliberative democracy (late twentieth century)

In August 1988 the American periodical *The Atlantic Monthly* published a remarkable article by one James Fishkin. It was only two pages long, but the content surprised many. It appeared just a few months before the presidential elections that brought George Bush Sr to power after an election battle against Michael Dukakis. Both candidates were nominated by their parties after a long series of primaries and caucuses up and down the nation. Since in the United States the earliest primaries are always held in the states of Iowa and New Hampshire and are the subject of intense media coverage, those states receive far more attention than they actually deserve. After all, whoever does well there will be given plenty of airtime and whoever does badly there might as well give up, since the financiers will pull out. Even before party supporters can take a close look at the candidates, the argument has largely been decided by the private laws of the media and sponsorship.

Is that right? Fishkin wondered. How democratic is it? As a young professor at the University of Texas, he was well versed in recent literature in his field. He was familiar, for example, with *Beyond Adversary Democracy* by political scientist Jane Mansbridge, which had been published a few years earlier. Mansbridge argues that there are two democratic traditions in America, adversary and unitary, one hostile and one respectful, one of parties doing battle and one of consultation between citizens. Of course Fishkin was also familiar with *Strong Democracy* by Benjamin Barber, published in 1984 and one of the most influential books on political theory in the final decades of the twentieth century. Barber distinguishes between strong and weak democracies and claims that today's conflict-ridden representative democracy is typical of the weak variety.

These were interesting times. John Rawls and Jürgen Habermas, two of the most important political philosophers of the post-war era, appealed for greater citizen participation in the conversation about what the future of our society should look like. Such a conversation could be rational and it would make for a fairer democracy at a time when more and more researchers were warning of the current system's limitations.

Shouldn't those new ideas be put into practice somewhere? In his article in *The Atlantic*, Fishkin proposed bringing together 1,500 citizens from all over America for two weeks, along with all the presidential candidates for the Republicans and the Democrats. The citizens would be able to listen to the candidates' plans and consult each other. Their deliberations would be shown on television, so that other citizens could also make well-founded choices. Fishkin deliberately adopted two aspects of Athenian democracy: participants would be chosen by lot and they would receive an allowance, to guarantee maximum diversity. 'Political equality stems from random sampling. In theory, every citizen has an equal chance of being chosen to participate.' The fair distribution of political opportunities: the Athenian ideal rises from the ashes, but what Fishkin had in mind with his sample was more than just another opinion poll: 'These polls model what the public is thinking when it is not thinking . . . A deliberative poll models what the public would think if it had a better chance to think about issues.'

The term 'deliberative democracy' was born, a democracy in which citizens don't merely vote for politicians but talk to each other and to experts. Deliberative democracy is a form of democracy in which collective deliberation is central and in which participants formulate concrete, rational solutions to social challenges based on information and reasoning. To prevent a few assertive participants from hijacking the group process, smaller subgroups are normally used, with professional moderators and the outline of a scenario. The literature on deliberative democracy has proliferated over recent years, but its inspiration is 2,500 years old. Fishkin wrote: 'This solution to the problem of combining political equality and deliberation actually dates back to ancient Athens, where deliberative microcosms of several hundred chosen by lot made many key decisions. With the demise of Athenian democracy, it fell into desuetude, then oblivion.'[93]

Fishkin made his proposal in all seriousness. He went in search of forms of organisation and of resources but had not reached a final analysis by the time of the 1992 election. How was everyone to be flown in? Where could they stay? Two weeks was a very long time and 1,500 citizens a great many. He adjusted his proposal, deciding that bringing six hundred people together for a weekend was more achievable and statistically still representative. After a few smaller deliberative projects he organised in Britain, he was ready by the time Bill Clinton and Bob Dole came to do battle in 1996. From 18 to 21 January, in Austin, Texas, the first deliberative opinion poll took place, called the National Issues Convention. Fishkin received support from, among others, American Airlines, Southwestern Bell, the city of Austin and PBS, America's Public Broadcasting Service, which between them donated four million dollars. PBS devoted more than four hours of broadcasting time to reporting on the initiative, so that the broader public could follow the deliberations between the citizens chosen and the presidential candidates. But despite this generous support, Fishkin faced a good many hostile reactions and several opinion-makers decried the proposal. Even before the event began, journalists all over America received copies of the magazine *Public Perspective* which warned against the initiative.[94] Citizens deliberating was considered to be impossible or at least undesirable, and in any case dangerous.

James Fishkin did not allow himself to lose heart. As an academic he wanted to find out what effect consultation like this would have on people. He had them fill in questionnaires – before, during and after the discussions – to see how their insights developed. Beforehand the participants were given files containing factual information, and they had a chance to speak to each other and to experts. Would that change their views? Observers were at any rate impressed: 'The sense of common purpose, the demonstration of mutual respect and the good sense of humour shared by most participants created a group atmosphere tolerant of conflicting views.'[95]

The conclusions of the objective soundings were radical and the difference between 'before' and 'after' turned out to be extremely striking. The consultation process had made the citizens significantly more competent and more sophisticated in their political judgements as they had learned to adjust their opinions and had become more aware of the complexity of political decision-making. It was the first time that scientific proof had been provided to show that ordinary individuals could become competent citizens, if they were given the right instruments. Fishkin believed his experiment offered opportunities for strengthening the democratic process by getting away from 'poll-driven mass democracy, from sound bites and democracy by slogans' to an 'authentic public voice'.[96]

The work of James Fishkin brought about a real deliberative turn in political science, and the fact that deliberative democracy can give a powerful boost to the ailing body of electoral-representative democracy is no longer doubted by any serious scholar. Citizen participation is not just a matter of being allowed to demonstrate, to strike, to sign petitions or to take part in other accepted forms of mobilisation in a public space.

It needs to be institutionally embedded. Fishkin has meanwhile organised dozens of deliberative opinion polls all over the world, often with impressive results.[97] Texas, the state where he has worked, drew lots on several occasions as a way of selecting people to come and talk about clean energy, not the most obvious subject for an oil state. As a result of deliberations between those citizens, the percentage of people who said they would be willing to pay more for wind-generated and solar power rose from 52 to 84%. Because of that increased support, by 2007 Texas had become the state with the most windmills in the United States, whereas ten years earlier it was way behind in that field. In Japan the discussion was about pensions, in Bulgaria about discrimination against the Roma, in Brazil about careers in public service, in China about urban policy, and so on, and each time the deliberations led to new legislation. Deliberative democracy also turned out to work in societies that were deeply divided, like that of Northern Ireland. Fishkin had Catholic and Protestant parents discuss reforms to education and it became obvious that people who were in the habit of speaking more about each other than with each other were in fact able to work out perfectly practical proposals.

Elsewhere too new models of citizen participation were sought after. Since the 1970s Germany has made use of *Planungszellen*, literally 'planning booths' and in 1986 Denmark introduced the Teknologi-rådet

(Technology Council), a body that works in parallel with parliament to allow citizen involvement in issues related to the consequences of new technology, such as the use of genetically modified organisms. France has since 1995 had a Commission Nationale du débat Public, which enables citizen participation in matters of the environment and infrastructure. Britain is set to work with Citizen Juries, and in 2000, Flanders established the Instituut Samenleving en Technology (Institute of Society and Technology) to involve citizens in technology policy. These are merely a few examples but the website participedia.net has information about hundreds of consultative projects set up over recent years, and the list is growing by the day.

Cities in particular proved fruitful ground for experiment and in New York residents spent two days deliberating what was to be built at Ground Zero, while in Manchester the subject under discussion was crime prevention. In the Brazilian city of Porto Alegre and countless other cities in South America, participative discussions take place in which citizens can become directly involved, deciding on the budgetary policy in their city. In Wenling, China, citizens chosen by lot are able to advise senior party officials about the priorities within large infrastructure projects. In South Rotterdam and Genk in 2013 a large sample of residents discussed the major socio-economic challenges of the future.

Participatory democracy is not limited to national or local democracy, however. The European Union adopted deliberative democracy on a large scale (Meeting of the Minds in 2005; European Citizens' Consultations in 2007 and 2009) and declared 2013 the Year of Citizens.

Irrespective of whether it's a matter of citizens' juries, mini-publics, consensus conferences, deliberative opinion polls, *Planungszellen*, *débats publics*, citizens' assemblies, people's parliaments or town hall meetings, the organisers have consistently found it worthwhile to hear the voices of citizens in between elections. Electoral-representative democracy has been enriched by a form of aleatoric-representative democracy.

Every deliberative project needs to decide what its citizens' panel will look like. If citizens can sign up on their own initiative, you can be certain they are motivated and will get involved. The disadvantage of self-selection, however, is that the panel will mainly feature articulate, highly educated white men aged over thirty, the so-called 'professional citizens', which is hardly ideal. If people are recruited by lot, there will be more diversity, more legitimacy, but also greater costs, as putting together a good, representative sample is expensive and the non-voluntary participants will have less prior knowledge and can more easily fall prey to a lack of interest. Self-selection increases efficiency, drawing lots increases legitimacy.

Sometimes an in-between form is adopted, with the drawing of lots followed by self-selection, or self-selection followed by the drawing of lots.

How not to do it was made clear in April 2008 when the Australian Prime Minister Kevin Rudd called together a thousand residents for a citizens' summit about Australia in 2020. He was in search of the 'best and brightest' in the country, a slogan that could have come from the late eighteenth century. Citizens had to nominate themselves, present a list of their own qualifications and submit a written account of how they would participate in the process. No compensation was available for travel expenses and overnight stays – and this in a country as vast as Australia. How many poor Aboriginal women from the north would have been eager to book a ticket to Canberra? It was a way of replacing the elected aristocracy not with a democracy but with a self-elected aristocracy, which would mean going from bad to worse. Citizen participation then becomes 'a meritocratic conclave'.[98]

Democratic innovation in practice: An international quest (2004–2013)

Of all the consultation processes of recent years there are five that I believe stand out as the most audacious and momentous. Moreover, they happened at a national level. Two took place in Canada, the others in the Netherlands,

FIGURE 4: Democratic innovation in certain Western countries

Country	Iceland 0.3 million	Ireland 6.4 million
Project	Constitutional assembly (Stjórnlagaþing á íslandi) 2010-2012	Convention on the Constitution (An Coinbhinsiún ar an mBunreacht) 2013
Task	New constitution	Eight articles of the constitution
Commissioned by	Parliament (Alþingi)	Parliament (Oireachtas)
Duration	2 years (3 phases)	1 year
Budget (€)	2.2 million	1.2 million
Number	25 citizens	100 citizens
Composition	Proportional distribution according to region and sex	66 lay members, 33 politicians (29 from the Republic, 4 from N. Ireland) 1 chair
Selection	By means of direct elections: 1. 522 candidates 2. 25 then elected 3. appointed by parliament	According to group: 1. chair appointed 2. citizens chosen by lot 3. politicians delegated
Remuneration	4 months' parliamentary salary per participant	all expenses reimbursed
Implementation	1. National forum: 1,000 citizens on values 2. Constitutional committee: advice of 7 politicians 3. Constitutional council: 25 citizens	1. Eight weekends with experts 2. Everyone invited to submit recommendations 3. Regional meetings 4. Plenary sessions via live streaming 5. Editing of recommendations
Report	*Proposal for a New Constitution for the Republic of Iceland* (July 2011)	*Reports and Recommendations from the Convention*
Mandate	Binding; referendum required	Binding; parliamentary majority required
Outcome	Referendum 2012: 2/3 majority on all points Parliament must approve twice, with elections in between.	Recommendations sent to parliament, which was asked to decide within four months whether there should be a referendum. Simple majority required at referendum.

British Columbia (Canada) 4.4 million	The Netherlands 16.7 million	Ontario (Canada) 12.9 million
Citizens' Assembly on Electoral Reform 2004	Citizens' Forum, Electoral system 2006	Citizens' Assembly on Electoral Reform 2006-2007
Reform of electoral system	Reform of electoral system	Reform of electoral system
Government	Government	Government
1 year	9 months (10 weekends)	9 months
4.1 million	5.1 million (excl. staff)	4.5 million
160 citizens	140 citizens	103 citizens
1 man & 1 woman from each of the 79 districts, plus 2 aboriginal members	Proportional distribution according to province and sex	1 citizen from each constituency, 52 women, 51 men, 1 aboriginal

Recruitment in three phases:
1. sortition: invitation to citizens chosen at random based on population lists
2. self-selection: those who choose to respond attend an informative meeting after which they confirm or decline participation
3. sortition: quota sampling from the group of candidates

110 euro per day, plus expenses and child care	400 euro per weekend	110 euro per day

The process consisted of three phases, each lasting 3 to 4 months:
1. Training phase, with experts
2. Consultation phase, with citizens; regional meetings
3. Decision-making phase and report

Making Every Vote Count (December 2004)	Met één stem meer keus (With one vote more choice) (December 2006)	One Ballot, Two Votes (May 2007)
Binding; referendum required	Non-binding	Binding; referendum required
Referendum 2005: 57.7% 2009: 39.9%	No referendum Discarded by government in 2008	Referendum 2007: 36.9%

Iceland and Ireland. They all came about over the past decade or so (in Ireland the process lasted until late 2013), they all had a temporary mandate and considerable government financing and they all concerned an extremely important subject: reform of electoral law or even the constitution. Here we were truly at the heart of democracy. This was something rather different from allowing citizens to join in discussions about windmills or corncobs.

Figure 4 brings together the basic data for each of those projects. I distinguish between two phases. The first ran from 2004 to 2009 and included citizens' forums in the Canadian provinces of British Columbia and Ontario and in the Netherlands, three projects that concerned reform to existing electoral law, or at least the development of a proposal for reform.

The second phase started in 2010 and is still under way. It includes the Constitutional Assembly in Iceland (Stjórnlagaþing á Íslandi) and the Convention on the Constitution in Ireland (An Coinbhinsiún ar an mBunreacht), two projects that considered proposals for changes to the constitution. In Ireland eight articles of the constitution were examined, in Iceland the entire text. It is no small matter to invite citizens to rewrite the constitution and it's surely no coincidence that two countries that took a real battering from the credit crisis of 2008 have dared to take democratic innovation so far. The bankruptcy of Iceland and the recession in Ireland severely tested the legitimacy of the prevailing model. Their governments had to do something to win back trust.

In 2004 British Columbia made the first move with the most ambitious deliberative process of modern times anywhere in the world. The Canadian province decided to entrust reform of its electoral law to a random sample of 160 citizens. Canada was still using a British electoral system that works according to the majority principle, whereby a candidate with a slight lead in a given constituency wins outright (winner takes all, in contrast to the proportional system). Was this fair? Participants in the citizens' assembly saw each other regularly for almost a year. Adjusting the rules of the electoral game is the kind of thing that political parties find hard to achieve by themselves, as rather than serving the common interest they continually have to ask themselves to what degree a new proposal will hurt them.

The idea of working with independent citizens seemed sensible in Ontario as well. The province had three times as many residents as British Columbia, but here too invitations were sent to a large, randomly chosen group of citizens who were on the electoral roll. Those interested were asked to attend an informative meeting where they could decide whether or not to take part. Out of that group of candidates a representative panel of 103 citizens was chosen by drawing lots: there were to be fifty-two women and fifty-one men, at least one of them would be a Native

Canadian and the age pyramid would be respected. Only the chair was appointed. Of the participants ultimately chosen by lot, seventy-seven turned out to have been born in Canada and twenty-seven were from elsewhere. They included childminders, bookkeepers, labourers, teachers, civil servants, entrepreneurs, computer programmers, students and care workers.

Although the Netherlands uses a form of proportional representation, the political party D66 has been appealing for years for improvements to the rules. When that party was engaged in negotiations to form a government in 2003 it persuaded its coalition partners to set up a Citizens' Forum to look at the electoral system, based on the Canadian precedent. Enthusiasm in the other parties was rather lukewarm, but if that was what it took to persuade D66 to enter the coalition, they could live with it. When D66 left the government as a result of early elections in 2006, the project was allowed to quietly fade away, so quietly in fact that most Dutch people, even regular newspaper readers, never even heard of it or can barely remember anything about it. That was a shame, since in Canada it produced some interesting work.[99]

In all these three cases, recruitment took place in three steps: 1) A large random sample of citizens was chosen from the electoral roll by the drawing of lots, and they received invitations by post. 2) A process of self-selection followed, so anyone interested could come to a meeting and put their name forward for the next stage. 3) From those candidates the final group was chosen, again by drawing lots, with attempts being made to achieve a balanced distribution of age, sex and so forth. It was therefore a system of sortition, followed by self-selection, followed by sortition.

In all three places, consultation lasted between nine and twelve months, during which time the participants had their first chance to talk to experts, look at documentation and become familiar with the subject matter. After that they consulted with other citizens and each other, then finally they formulated a concrete proposal for a new electoral law. (We should note, incidentally, that citizens in Ontario chose a different electoral model from those in British Columbia: deliberation is not manipulation in a predetermined direction.)

What is striking to anyone who reads the online reports of those Canadian and Dutch citizen-parliaments is the degree of nuance in arguments for a technically refined alternative. Anyone who doubts whether ordinary citizens chosen at random are capable of making sensible and rational decisions really ought to read those reports. Fishkin's findings were confirmed once again.

However, what also becomes obvious is that none of the three projects exerted a real influence on policy. Sensible input but hardly any concrete output? Right. In all three cases the proposal from the citizens' assembly had to be endorsed in a referendum. It seems drawing lots was still too unfamiliar a democratic instrument to enjoy intrinsic legitimacy, rather as if the verdict of an American jury needed to be ratified by referendum. But that's simply how it was, and as a consequence, the work of dozens of citizens carried out over many months was to be judged by the population in a few seconds. In British Columbia 57.7% of citizens voted in favour, a large proportion but not quite enough to reach the required threshold of 60%. (In a fresh referendum in 2009 enthusiasm shrank to 39.9%.) In Ontario only 36.9% of citizens voted in favour while in the Netherlands Prime Minister Jan Peter Balkenende's cabinet decided not to adopt the advice of the Citizens' Forum, which it had financed to the tune of more than five million euros.

Democratic renewal is a slow process so the reasons for the ultimate failure of that process in Canada and the Netherlands should prove extremely instructive. The causes are several and worth noting: 1) Citizens who voted in the referendum had not been following the deliberations so their raw opinion in the voting booth was in stark contrast to the informed opinion of participants.[100] 2) Citizens' forums are merely temporary institutions with a limited mandate, so their voice carried less weight than that of formal, established bodies. 3) Political parties often had an interest in discrediting a proposal or simply ignoring it, since reform to the electoral system would have cost them power (in the Netherlands the government decided not even to hold a referendum but simply to ditch the proposals).[101] 4) Commercial media in Canada were often extremely hostile to the citizens' assemblies, irrespective of the content of the proposals, while in Ontario the press was actually hysterically negative.[102] 5) The citizens' forums often had no seasoned spokespeople or adequate campaign budgets available; the verdict was pronounced in the media, but the money available was spent on the actual work rather than marketing. 6) Referendums about complex proposals for reform will perhaps always work to the advantage of the No camp – if you don't know, say No! In the case of the European Constitution it was sufficient for opponents to sow doubt so the Yes camp had to work harder and put more effort into communicating. The question we should ask is whether referendums are a suitable way of taking decisions on complex matters.[103]

Over recent decades the referendum has often been presented as an effective means of reforming democracy. In a time of individualisation and with organised civil society weighing less heavily than it once did, many thought it would be useful to ask the opinion of the population directly, although this enthusiasm has cooled somewhat since the referendums on the European Constitution in the Netherlands, France and Ireland. They still enjoy great popularity, as was shown by the holding of referendums on independence in Catalonia and Scotland, and on Britain's membership of the European Union. Referendums and deliberative democracy are similar in the sense that they turn directly to the ordinary citizen to ask his or her opinion, but other than that they are completely at odds with each other. In a referendum you ask everyone to vote on a subject that usually only a few know anything about, whereas in a deliberative project you ask a representative sample of people to consider a subject about which they are given all possible information. A referendum very often reveals people's gut reactions; deliberations reveal enlightened public opinion.

Citizens' assemblies may do great work, but sooner or later they have to declare their findings, which is always a difficult process, because the seclusion of civil consultation is suddenly exposed to the glaring light of the public arena. As it turns out, the fiercest opponents consistently come from the camps of the political parties and the commercial media, a phenomenon as widespread as it is intriguing. Where does that hostility come from? A question many academics and activists are asking themselves. Whereas civil society often has a positive attitude to citizen participation – if only because trades unions, employers' organisations, youth movements, women's organisations and other players in social life have been engaged in it for more than a century – the press and politicians often tend to be scornful. Is it because they are used to serving as the gatekeepers of public opinion and do not want to give up that privilege? That is almost certainly part of the story. Because press and politicians act within the old electoral-representative system they may find it difficult to cope with newer forms of democracy.

Another possibility that cannot be excluded is that those who are accustomed to working top-down find it hard to cope with what comes from the bottom up.

But there are other factors at play. Political parties are always anxious about their voters and although we are familiar with the fact that many citizens distrust their politicians, the idea that politicians can be just as distrustful of their citizens is still new to us. Recall the research by Peter Kanne, which showed that nine out of ten politicians are suspicious of the population. If politicians collectively believe that the population by definition thinks differently from the way they do, then we should not be surprised if they are primed to be sceptical about citizen participation.

The media have their doubts as well. Deliberative processes with citizens chosen by lot are often intense experiences for the participants but they do not fit easily into the format of contemporary reporting. They are slow, there are no leading figures, no familiar faces and no major conflicts. Citizens simply sit at round tables talking, Post-its and marker pens to hand, with little to attract an audience. Parliamentary democracy is theatre and sometimes produces great TV, but deliberative democracy has little drama and is difficult to shape into a story. In Britain, Channel 4 once broadcast a series called *The People's Parliament*, which employed James Fishkin as an advisor and used hundreds of citizens, chosen by lot, to debate controversial subjects such as youth crime and laws on striking. The series was abandoned after a few episodes as it simply did not grab the viewer's interest.[104] This too helps to explain the reservations in the media.

Iceland took account of the unfortunate outcomes of the Canadian and Dutch experiments, and to forestall the danger that the work of a citizens' panel might be ditched before it had a proper chance, far-reaching adjustments were made. For a start, instead of choosing some hundred to 160 citizens by lot, only twenty-five took part, and they were selected by voting. Candidates had to produce thirty signatures. A total of 522 people came forward. The rest of the population went to the ballot box to choose the team of twenty-five. (As a result of squabbling between the official political parties, the vote was later declared null and void, at which point the parliament selected the group itself, but that is beside the point. The philosophy was that the constitutional forum must be elected.) Secondly, there was a desire to avoid the activities of this one small group lacking legitimacy among citizens and politicians. Thousands of citizens were therefore asked to discuss the principles and values of the new constitution beforehand, while seven politicians put together preliminary advice in a 700-page document. This was intended to take the wind out of the sails of later critics. The organisers also deliberately chose not to shut the team of twenty-five up in a black box from which it would emerge after months of internal consultation with a ready-made constitution. Instead, while compiling its new document, the assembly posted provisional versions of constitutional clauses on the website every week. The feedback that came in via Facebook, Twitter and other media led to newer versions that were also placed online and so on, the process enriched by almost four thousand comments. Transparency and consultation were key, the *International Herald Tribune* describing it as the first constitution to be produced by crowdsourcing.

All this had its effect. When the proposed constitution was put to the citizens of Iceland in a referendum on 20 October 2012, two-thirds voted in favour. To an additional question that had arisen during deliberations by the constitutional assembly, namely whether the natural resources of the island that were not in private hands should become the property of the nation, no fewer than 83% answered in the affirmative.[105]

Even though after several years parliamentary approval has yet to be given, the Iceland adventure is without doubt the most impressive example of deliberative democracy thus far. Was it the great openness of the whole process that made it so successful or was it the decision to elect the participants rather than drawing lots? It is difficult to say. The election certainly brought competent people to the fore, and this was good for efficiency as within four months a new constitution had been written. However, it was less good for legitimacy. How diverse is a constitutional assembly of twenty-five people if seven of them are in positions of leadership (at universities, museums or trades unions) and of the rest five are professors or lecturers, four are media figures, four artists, two lawyers and one a clergyman? Even the father of singer Björk, a prominent trade unionist, managed to get a place on it. There was just one farmer.[106] The composition of the panel was perhaps the weakest link, methodologically speaking, in the entire Icelandic consultative process. The impressive transparency of the process may have contributed more to the mass approval of the proposed constitution than the composition of the citizens' panel. So the question remains: would a team of citizens chosen purely by lot, with more time and the same degree of openness, be able to put together a constitution that scored just as highly in a referendum?

That question was put on the table a short time later in Ireland. The Convention on the Constitution that began work in January 2013 also drew lessons from earlier democratic experiments. Its conclusions were to involve politicians far more intensively (as in Iceland), but to continue selecting citizens by drawing lots (unlike in Iceland). The Irish also decided that the chances of success and implementation would be greater if they invited politicians to become involved in the process at an early stage. In this they went much further than the people of Iceland. Rather than a handful of them being available to give preliminary advice, they made a conscious decision to bring politicians and citizens together throughout. Sixty-six citizens and thirty-three politicians, from both the Republic and Northern Ireland, including for example Gerry Adams, spent a year in consultation. It might seem strange that a process of citizen participation would ask famous names from political parties to speak, with all their rhetorical talent and knowledge of the issues, but that decision was designed to hasten implementation of the decisions made, reduce the fear of citizen participation among politicians and prevent scornful reactions from political parties at a later stage. The deliberative process can sometimes have a remarkable effect on those taking part, politicians losing their distrust of citizens, just as citizens lose their distrust of politicians. Citizen participation can reinforce mutual trust, although of course there is always the danger that politicians will hold sway. We will have to await analysis of the Irish model, but if the process is properly designed, the disproportionate weight of some participants will be obviated by internal checks and balances, by breaking up into subgroups, for example, and spreading decision-making widely.

The Irish also opted resolutely for the drawing of lots, and their Constitutional Convention built on We the Citizens, a successful project at University College Dublin with citizens chosen by sortition. An independent research bureau put together the random group of sixty-six, taking account of age, sex and origin (Republic or Northern

Ireland). The diversity this produced was helpful when it came to discussing such sensitive subjects as gay marriage, the rights of women or the ban on blasphemy in the current constitution. However, they did not do all this alone, as in Ireland, too, participants listened to experts and received input from other citizens (more than a thousand contributions came in on the subject of gay marriage). The decisions made by the convention did not have the force of law, incidentally. The recommendations first had to be passed by the two chambers of the Irish Parliament, then by the government and then in a referendum. There were many locks to pass through, therefore, since in the second phase of citizens' forums, as in the first, there is a fear that drawing lots may create turbulent waters.

However, on 22 May 2015 the people of Ireland voted in a national referendum in favour of a change to the constitution that would allow gay marriage. The Yes camp received no less than 62% of the votes. The referendum was held after the Constitutional Convention recommended changing the constitution in this respect by a majority of 79%. I can think of no better example of how deliberative democracy can make a difference to practical reality. It was the first time anywhere in the world in modern times that a discussion among citizens chosen by lot led to an adjustment in a country's constitution.[107]

So in supposedly Catholic Ireland, the introduction of gay marriage took place in comparative tranquillity, partly because of citizen participation, whereas supposedly libertarian France saw a year of intense political unrest surrounding exactly the same subject. More than 300,000 people joined demonstrations, marching through the streets of Paris. There the citizen was given no say.

Democratic innovation in the future: Allotted assemblies

I have described in some detail these examples from Canada, the Netherlands, Iceland and Ireland because they represent particularly exciting experiments in democratic innovation. But even though they took place on a large scale and were about essential issues, the mainstream media outside those countries rarely reported on them and as a result much knowledge and experience did not reach a broader international audience. The delay, however, has not stopped others from thinking further ahead. Democracy advances at different rates and while politicians remain hesitant, the media distrustful and citizens uninformed, academics and activists are already way ahead of them. It is their task, as Belgian philosopher Philippe Van Parijs has put it, 'to be right too soon'.[108] When John Stuart Mill argued in the mid nineteenth century that women deserved to be given the vote, his contemporaries said he was mad.

Knowing they could expect condescension or even howls of derision, various authors over past decades have advocated anchoring sortition in democracy institutionally and constitutionally. They were of the view that it should not remain confined to one-off projects but that citizens chosen by lot should become components of the state apparatus. How that could be made possible was a matter for discussion, but a popular proposal was the idea of using the drawing of lots to compile one of the legislative organs. To date more than twenty such scenarios have been put forward.[109] Every one of these authors concluded that a randomly composed parliament could make democracy more legitimate and efficient, more legitimate because it would revive the ideal of the equitable distribution of political opportunities

FIGURE 5: Proposals for allotted legislative assemblies

Country	USA	UK
Name	Representative House	House of Peers
Function	to replace House of Representatives	to replace House of Lords
Size	435	600
Composition	anonymously chosen by lot from existing lists for jury service	1. lots drawn from electoral roll 2. self-selection 3. sortition according to quota (sex, region); plus several party politicians
Duration	3 years (but overlapping)	1-4 years
Remuneration	generous	at least equal to current parliamentarians' pay plus reasonable compensation to employers
Mandate	- to initiate laws - to evaluate laws initiated by the Senate	purely to evaluate legislation drawn up by the Commons (for clarity, effectiveness, constitutionality)
Author	Callenbach & Phillips 1985	Barnett & Carty 1998
See also	Burnheim 1985; Leib 2005; O'Leary 2006	Barnett & Carty 2008; Zakaras 2010

and more efficient because the new representatives of the people would not lose themselves in party-political tugs of war, electoral games, media battles or legislative haggling. They would be able to concentrate simply on the common interest. I will look at five of the most important proposals (see figure 5).[110]

In 1985 American authors Ernest Callenbach and Michael Phillips suggested transforming the US House of Representatives into a Representative House, the 435 representatives of the people no longer being elected but

UK	France	EU
House of Commons	**Troisième Assemblée**	**House of Lots**
to replace current House of Commons	to exist alongside Sénat and Assemblée nationale	to exist alongside European Parliament
		200
sortition, given adequate age, insight and education	sortition among volunteer candidates	sortition among all EU citizens, proportionate according to member state; participation compulsory
1-10 years		2.5 years (max. 1 term)
gonorous	at least equal to that of *députés* or *sénateurs* + training and administration	to be made financially and organisationally very attractive
purely to evaluate legislation	long-term issues: ecology, society, electoral law, constitution	- initiate - advise - veto
Sutherland 1998	Sintomer 2011	Buchstein 2009
Sutherland 2011		Buchstein & Hein 2010

instead chosen by lot. If such an idea seems to be far-fetched, think again. It would be a mistake to suppose that these authors are fantasists. Ernest Callenbach made his name the year before with his book *Ecotopia*, which sold a million copies, and many of his audacious insights of those days are now generally accepted. Michael Phillips was a banker who had published books including *The Seven Laws of Money* and *Honest Business*. In the 1960s he was the brain behind MasterCard.

The current, purely electoral system was in their view not representative, and too susceptible to corruption, and the power of big money weighed too heavily. Selection by lot could help. Random citizens would be taken from existing lists used for jury service (in the United States these are more inclusive than electoral rolls) to serve as Members of Parliament for three years. Their pay would be in keeping, since there was a need to ensure that poor people wanted to participate, rich people would be willing to interrupt their jobs and those with busy careers could make time. To guarantee continuity, the House would not gather in its entirety on a single day but in instalments, one-third each year. Its powers would be no different from those of the current House: to propose legislation to the Senate and to evaluate legislation proposed by the Senate.

It is striking that Callenbach and Phillips did not advocate doing away with elections altogether. They felt it was useful to have a Senate with elected citizens and a House with citizens chosen purely by lot. Representation had to come about both by electoral and by aleatoric means. 'We believe that the idea of direct representation is not quixotic. Once it is widely understood, it will have the same overwhelming appeal to fairness and justice that motivated extensions of the suffrage.'[111]

Their suggestion has been refined over recent years by various authors, and there were proposals for the United Kingdom as well. Anthony Barnett and Peter Carty believed that the House of Lords, the only senate in the Western world in which membership is still hereditary in some cases, must be democratised. Barnett is the founder of the website openDemocracy and he writes regularly for the *Guardian* while Carty writes for various quality British newspapers (*Guardian, Independent, Independent on Sunday, Financial Times* and so on). Unlike their American colleagues they want to see the upper house chosen by lot, and not the House of Commons. Nor do they believe that this allotted body should have the right to initiate laws; supervision of legislation coming from the lower house must be sufficient. The new House of Lords, which they rename the House of Peers, would then check that the legislation is clear, effective and constitutional.[112] Of course they realised that this was a radical plan, but a democracy does need prospects. They write that the life of every important idea goes through three phases: 'First it is ignored. Next it is ridiculed. Then it becomes accepted wisdom.'[113]

Keith Sutherland, a researcher attached to the University of Exeter who identifies himself as a conservative, believes it should be the other way round. The House of Lords should remain the House of Lords with the House of Commons transformed into an allotted chamber, as in the American proposal. He also believes that generous pay is important and follows his British colleagues in proposing not to give the right of initiative to the allotted house. He does wonder whether minimal conditions should be attached regarding age, education and competence. As a conservative he suggests that those eligible should be over forty as the needs of younger members of the population already receive enough attention, he believes, in the mass media, party politics and marketing. Whatever might be thought of that, the bottom line is clear: 'Sortition is an indispensible component of any system of government that seeks to call itself democratic.'[114]

In France political scientist Yves Sintomer proposed not replacing the Assemblée or the Sénat with an allotted chamber but instead enriching the system with a new chamber. Members of this 'Third House' would be chosen by lot from among volunteer candidates and he too points to the importance of suitable payment and information provision. Staff would be available to support representatives, as is now the case with elected *députés*. He does not say who should have what rights, but he proposes that the Third

Chamber should concern itself with subjects that require long-term planning (ecology, social issues, electoral law and the constitution). This, after all, is the dimension that all too often goes by the board in the current model.[115]

German professor Hubertus Buchstein also advocates setting up an additional chamber, not at a national but at a supranational level. There is a need for a second European Parliament, he says, this time made up of citizens chosen by lot. He calls it the House of Lots. Its two hundred participants would be selected by sortition from the total adult population of the European Union, spread equitably over the member states, for a term of two and a half years. Participation would be compulsory, short of some unavoidable obstacle, and he too believes that the financial and organisational conditions must be such that no one has any good reason to decline. Unlike the British authors he thinks that the EU's House of Lots should be able to initiate legislation, as well as having the right to advise and even to veto. These are far-reaching measures, but Buchstein is of the opinion that 'a deliberative pressure to decide' is necessary to counter Europe's democratic deficit.[116] Only with deliberative pressure of this kind can the Union hope to achieve efficient and transparent decision-making.

What we notice if we put these various proposals side by side is that first of all they concern very large entities: France, the United Kingdom, the US or the EU. The time has passed when sortition seemed suitable only for city states and mini-states. Second, despite considerable differences of opinion, there is a consensus regarding the term of office (ideally several years) and the remuneration (ideally generous). Third, the unequally distributed competencies of citizens must be obviated by training and by the support of experts, as already happens in parliaments today. Fourth, the body selected by lot must never be seen as separate from an elected body but complementary to it. Fifth, all these proposals advocate using sortition for just one legislative chamber.

Blueprint for a democracy based on sortition

In the spring of 2013, the academic periodical *Journal of Public Deliberation* published a fascinating contribution by American researcher Terrill Bouricius. In a previous life Bouricius had worked for twenty years as an elected politician in the state of Vermont and he asked himself how achievable earlier proposals were. Could the replacement of an elected chamber with an allotted chamber give democracy a new boost by injecting more support and more energy? His question was particularly pertinent. Ideally there would indeed be a European Parliament, based on sortition, that was representative of the entire EU, but how many women running baker's shops in Lithuanian villages would close their shutters for several years to take their seats in Strasbourg in the House of Lots? How many young engineers in Malta would abandon their promising building projects for three years because Europe had drawn lots and happened to select them? How many unemployed people in the British Midlands would leave pub and friends for years to tinker around with legislation alongside people they'd never met? And even if they wanted to do it, would they be any good? Such a parliament might be more legitimate, because more representative, but would it also be more efficient or would most of those chosen by lot come up with all kinds of excuses for not going, so that the representation of the people again became a task for highly educated men? Strengthening democracy by drawing lots to form an assembly sounds good, but it comes up against countless objections. You want everyone to have a say, but that is to risk new forms of elitism. How can the ideal be reconciled with the practicalities? That was the question with which Bouricius struggled.

He returned to Athenian democracy, studied its workings and asked himself what its modern application would look like. In Athenian democracy sortition was typically used not merely for a single institution but for a whole series, thereby creating a system of checks and balances, one such body keeping an eye on the other. 'The Council of 500 set the agenda, and prepared preliminary decrees and resolutions for the Assembly to consider, but could not pass laws. The passage of a decree by the People's Assembly could be over-ruled by a People's Court, but these Courts could not pass laws themselves.' The decision-making process was therefore spread across several institutions (see Figure 2B). This might seem to be a bit of a rigmarole, but it had clear advantages:

> The Athenian separation of powers between multiple randomly selected bodies and the self-selected attendees of the People's Assembly achieved three important goals that our modern elected legislatures do not: 1) the legislative bodies were relatively descriptively representative of the citizenry; 2) they were highly resistant to corruption and undue concentration of political power; and 3) the opportunity to participate – and make decisions – was spread broadly throughout the relevant population.[117]

*

Working with several allotted bodies ('multi-body sortition' as Bouricius calls it) ensured more legitimacy and more efficiency.

How could such a system work today? In Figure 6 I have tried to present Bouricius' model in diagram form. I have done so based on his article, supplemented by an earlier study and by email correspondence with him and his colleague David Schecter.

In reality, says Bouricius, you require as many as six different organs because there is a need to reconcile conflicting interests, and being an expert in the field of democratic innovation, he knows what a challenge this is. You want sortition to provide a large, representative sample, but you also know that it's easier to work in small groups. You want rapid rotation to promote participation, but you also know that longer mandates produce better work. You want to let everyone take part who wishes to do so, but you also know that this means highly educated and articulate citizens will be over-represented. You want citizens to be able to consult each other, but you also know that this presents the danger of group thinking, the tendency to be too quick to find a consensus. You want to give as much power as possible to an allotted body, but you also know that some individuals will put too much pressure on the group process, producing arbitrary outcomes.

These five dilemmas are familiar to anyone who has ever worked with alternative forms of consultation. They concern the ideal size of the group, the ideal duration, the ideal selection method, the ideal consultation method and the ideal group dynamic. Well, according to Bouricius there is no ideal, so better just give up the quest for one and set about designing a model that consists of several organs. That way the advantages of various options can reinforce each other and the disadvantages weaken each other.

Instead of giving all the power to a single allotted body, legislative work is best split into a number of phases.

In the first phase the agenda needs to be set. In Bouricius' system this happens in the Agenda Council,

FIGURE 6: Multi-body sortition: blueprint for a democracy based on sortition (numbers are hypothetical)

AGENDA COUNCIL – *compiles the agenda, chooses topics for legislation*

Size: 150-400 people, possibly in subcommittees

Composition: chosen by lot from among volunteers

Duration: full time

Rotation: 3 years (1/3 each year), no extension

Remuneration: salary

INTEREST PANELS – *propose topic-related legislation*

Size: 12 per panel, number of panels unlimited

Composition: volunteers, who put their names forward

Frequency: as often as they desire

Duration: panel ends at deadline

Remuneration: none

REVIEW PANELS – *compile legislation according to the input of interest panels and experts*

Size: 150, divided up into separate panels; each panel empowered for a single domain; participants do not choose their panel but are allocated to it

Composition: chosen by lot from among volunteers

Frequency: full time

Rotation: 3 years (1/3 each year), no extension

Remuneration: salary and support

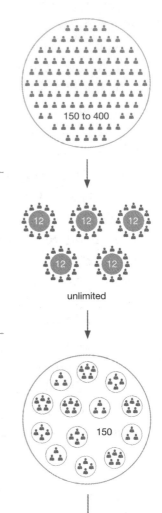

POLICY JURY – *votes on legislation; secret ballot after public presentations*

Size: 400, purely plenary

Composition: chosen by lot from among all adult citizens, participation compulsory

Frequency: when legislation needs to be voted on

Duration: one day or several days

Remuneration: payment per day plus travel or other expenses

RULES COUNCIL – *decides on rules and procedures of legislative work*

Size: c. 50 people

Composition: chosen by lot from among volunteers (possibly former participants)

Frequency: full time (at least at the start)

Rotation: 3 years (1/3 each year), no extension

Remuneration: salary

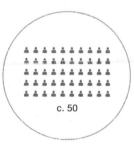

OVERSIGHT COUNCIL – *regulates the legislative process and deals with complaints*

Size: c. 20 people

Composition: chosen by lot from among volunteers

Frequency: full time

Rotation: 3 years (1/3 each year), no extension

Remuneration: salary

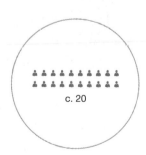

143

a very broad organ whose members are chosen by lot from those who have put themselves forward (rather in the way the Athenian people's courts worked). The Agenda Council designates topics but does not develop them further, as it doesn't have that power. Citizens who don't belong to this body but want to draw attention to a specific subject can use their right to petition, and if they can collect enough signatures their issue will be dealt with.

In a second phase, all kinds of Interest Panels are brought into play. There may be just a few of them, or there may be a hundred. Interest Panels are groups of twelve citizens that can each propose a bill, or part of a bill. Members are neither elected nor chosen by lot, they simply volunteer to help think about that particular subject. Such a panel may have twelve members who don't know each other and have no common purpose, but they might equally well be a lobby. This is not a problem as they do not have the last word and must take into account the fact that their proposal will be evaluated by others. Working with Interest Panels ensures that those who have relevant experience can combine their expertise for use in drawing up concrete policy proposals which will help make the system efficient. Imagine traffic safety is on the agenda. Those involved might be neighbourhood organisations, cyclists' federations, bus conductors, people from the transport sector, parents of children killed in car accidents, motorists' organisations and so on.

In a third phase, all these proposals are put before a Review Panel, of which there is one for each policy area. Proposals concerning traffic safety, for example, come before the Review Panel that concerns itself with mobility. These panels are best compared with parliamentary committees as they do not have the right to initiate legislation nor to vote on its adoption, merely doing the work in between (as did the Council of 500 in Athens). Using the input received from the Interest Panels, they organise hearings, invite experts and work on developing legislation. All the Review Panels combined, Bouricius proposes, will have 150 members, chosen by lot from among citizens who have put themselves forward, and their job will carry great responsibility. Members take their seats for three years, they work full time and are paid appropriately, receiving an amount comparable to that of a parliamentary salary. They are not all replaced at once, but in phases, fifty seats per working year.

To avoid all power being concentrated in the Review Panels there is a fourth organ, a very important one. Legislation is put before a Policy Jury, the most unusual organ in Bouricius' plan. It has no permanent members. Every time a vote on a piece of legislation is needed, four hundred citizens are chosen by lot to come together for one day or in certain cases for several days, a week at the most. Crucially, lots are drawn from the entire adult population and not just those who have put themselves forward as candidates, so in this sense it is more like jury service for a criminal trial. To ensure the body is as representative as possible, whoever is chosen has to appear unless he or she has a valid excuse, so for this reason participants are well rewarded for their attendance. The Policy Jury hears the various legislative proposals put together by the Review Panel, listens to a formal presentation of arguments for and against, and then votes on them in a secret ballot. So there is no further discussion, no party discipline, no group pressure, no tactical voting, no political haggling and no back-scratching. Everyone votes according to their conscience, according to what he or she feels best serves the general interest in the long term. To avoid charismatic speakers influencing the mood, the legislative proposals are presented by neutral staff members. Because the verdict is that of a good cross section of society as a whole, the decisions of the Policy Jury have the force of law.

To streamline the process, Terrill Bouricius proposes a further two organs, a Rules Council and an Oversight Council, both again chosen by lot. The first is responsible for developing procedures for the drawing of lots, for hearings and for voting. The second ensures that civil servants follow the correct procedures and deal with any complaints. These two councils therefore have a meta-political function, compiling and safeguarding the rules of the game. The Rules Council could be chosen by lot from among people who have already served in one of the other allotted bodies and who therefore know the ins and outs of the procedures.

What makes this model particularly attractive is its capacity to evolve, as nothing is fixed beforehand. 'A key factor is that all of this would only be a starting design,' Bouricius wrote in an email,

> but it would evolve as the Rules Council deemed optimal. The one rule I would like to somehow make permanent is that the Rules Council cannot grant themselves more power. Perhaps an initial rule should be that rules changes that affect the Rules Council itself can only go into effect after there has been a 100% turn-over in membership. Also, once the system is in place for a while, I can imagine limiting the lottery pool for the Rules Council to volunteers who have served on some other randomly selected body previously.[118]

Instead of tracing everything out in minute detail beforehand therefore, he is developing a 'self-learning system'. One striking thing about this blueprint is how the eternal quest for democracy – for a favourable balance between efficiency and legitimacy – is given shape here in a system based purely on drawing lots. The fact that citizens can voluntarily put their names forward for five of the six organs would definitely help to inject vigour into the system (for the Interest Panels they do not even need to be selected, as anyone who wishes to can take part). But the fact that the ultimate verdict, the last word in the decision-making process, rests with the representative sample of the Policy Jury is essential for legitimacy. In a nutshell: anyone who feels capable of serving society is given the chance to get involved in the discussion, but it is the community as a whole that ultimately decides.

This balance between maintaining support and acting decisively would not have seemed possible in the late eighteenth century. The American and French revolutionaries thought state business too important to be left to the people and by opting for an elected aristocracy they gave priority to efficiency over legitimacy. Nowadays we are paying the price for that. Discontent is rife and the legitimacy of the electoral-representative system is being noisily called into question.

Bouricius' proposal is exceptionally exciting. It is a stimulating example of how democracy could be set up in a completely different way. It takes its inspiration from ancient Athens but does not simply adopt those procedures wholesale without further thought. It is founded upon recent academic research into deliberative democracy and experiments with the drawing of lots, so it recognises the potential traps of specific formulas. It develops a system of checks and balances to avoid those traps and to prevent any concentration of power, and above all it brings politics back to the citizens. The elitist distinction between governors and governed is abolished completely, returning us to the Aristotelian ideal of having people alternate between ruling and being ruled.

*

So where do we go from here? Brilliant historical research has been carried out, political philosophers have done wonderful work, we have a mass of inspiring practical examples and several refined proposals are on the table, of which Bouricius' is particularly promising. What is the next step?

Bouricius' model is designed to evolve, but it can start to do so only once it becomes a reality, and how the transition from the current system to his system could be effected remains unclear. In an earlier piece, written with his colleague David Schecter, he suggested that the model could be applied 'in a variety of ways':

1. Make one law (like the British Columbia Citizens' Assembly).
2. Make all laws within one issue area (for example, an area that is so controversial that elected officials would actually prefer to delegate it to citizens, or where legislators have a conflict of interest, as in term limits, legislative salaries, or election law).
3. Enhance the deliberative quality of an initiative and referendum process.
4. Replace one elected house of a bicameral legislature.
5. Carry out the entire legislative process in place of an elected legislature.[119]

What if we were to see those five possible applications as five steps in a historic transformation? Start hesitantly and end enthusiastically, a process that has in a sense already started. Phase 1 happened in Canada, phase 2 in Ireland and phase 3 has been going on longest. Phases 4 and 5 – yes, those are of course the great challenges and we haven't got anywhere with them as yet. It's definitely too soon for the full application of Bouricius' programme (phase 5). Unless they face the threat of revolution, political parties will not be quick to dissolve themselves overnight in order to make multi-body sortition possible, but the time for phase 4 is approaching.

Timely appeal for a bi-representative system

Democracy is like clay, it's shaped by its time and the concrete forms it takes are always moulded by historical circumstances. As a type of government to which consultation is central, it is extremely sensitive to the means of communication available. The democracy of ancient Athens was formed in part by the culture of the spoken word, and the electoral-representative democracy of the nineteenth and twentieth centuries thrived in the era of the printed word (the newspaper and other one-direction media such as radio, television and internet 1.0). Today, however, we are in an era of articulacy, of hyper-fast, decentralised communication, which has created new forms of political involvement. What kind of democracy is appropriate to it?[120]

How should the government deal with all those articulate citizens who stand shouting from the sidelines?

First, with pleasure rather than suspicion, because behind all the anger both online and offline lies something positive, namely engagement. It may be a gift wrapped in barbed wire, but indifference would be far worse. Second, by learning to let go, not wanting to do everything on the citizen's behalf, because the citizen is not a child. At the start of the third millennium, relationships are more horizontal.

Doctors have had to learn to deal with patients who've already looked up their symptoms on the internet. At first that seemed problematic, now it turns out to be a blessing because empowerment can assist recovery, and the same applies to politics when authority changes. Once you had authority and were allowed to speak, now you gain authority by speaking. Leadership is no longer a matter of taking decisions on behalf of the people but of setting processes in train along with the people. Treat responsible citizens as ballot fodder and they'll behave like ballot fodder, but treat them as adults and they'll behave like adults. The bond between government and the governed is no longer the same as that between parents and children. We are all adults now and politicians would do well to look past the barbed wire, trust the citizens, take their emotions seriously and value their experience. Invite them in, give them power and because it will always be fair, take all their names and draw lots.

I believe the systemic crisis of democracy can be remedied by giving sortition a fresh chance. The drawing of lots is not a miracle cure, not a perfect recipe, any more than elections ever were, but it can correct a number of the faults in the current system. Drawing lots is not irrational, it is arational, a consciously neutral procedure whereby political opportunities can be distributed fairly and discord avoided. The risk of corruption reduces, election fever abates and attention to the common good increases. Citizens chosen by lot may not have the expertise of professional politicians, but they add something vital to the process: freedom. After all, they don't need to be elected or re-elected.

For this reason it is worthwhile in this phase of history to entrust legislative power not only to elected citizens but to citizens chosen by lot as well. If we can rely on the principle of sortition in the criminal justice system, why not rely on it in the legislative system? It will restore a good deal of peace. Elected citizens (our politicians) will not be driven by commercial and social media alone, they will be flanked by a second assembly to which election fever and viewing figures are totally irrelevant, an assembly where the common interest and the long term still come first, an assembly of citizens in which it is truly possible to have a conversation, not because those citizens are thought to be better than the rest but because circumstances will bring the best in them to the fore.

Democracy is not government by the best in our society, because such a thing is called an aristocracy, elected or not. That is one option, but then let's change here and now what we call it. Democracy, by contrast, flourishes precisely by allowing a diversity of voices to be heard. It's all about having an equal say, an equal right to determine what political action is taken. As American philosopher Alex Guerrero put it recently: 'Each person in a political jurisdiction should have an equal right to participate substantively in determining what political actions will be taken by that political institution.'[121] In short, it's about governing and being governed, about government of the people, for the people and, at last, also by the people.

Yet the water is still deep. 'Citizens can't do this!' 'Politics is difficult!' 'Idiots in power!' 'Plebs at the helm, beware!' And so on. Before going any further we need to take a look at the most common argument against sortition, the supposed incompetence of the non-elected. This criticism has a positive aspect as it proves that many people cherish the quality of their democracy. Woe betide the country where democratic innovation raises no objections, for it is a place where concern has been swallowed by the waves and apathy reigns. Woe betide the country that cannot have a tranquil conversation about the future of democracy, for there hysteria prevails.

The general panic engendered by the idea of sortition shows the degree to which two centuries of the electoral-representative system and hierarchical thinking has succeeded in firmly fixing in people's minds a belief that affairs of state can be looked after only by exceptional individuals. I'll address a few of my opponents' arguments:

- It is important to realise that the reasons nowadays put forward for not choosing citizens by lot are often identical to the reasons once put forward for not allowing peasants, workers or women to vote. Then, too, opponents claimed it would mark the end of democracy.
- A body of elected representatives undoubtedly has more technical competencies within it than a body chosen by lot. But everyone is an expert on their own life. What is the use of a parliament full of highly educated lawyers if few of them know the price of bread? Sortition produces a legislature that includes a greater cross section of society.
- Those elected are not always particularly competent either. If they were, why would they need to have staffs, researchers and human resources departments at their disposal, and why are ministers able to move to a different ministry from one day to the next? Surely they can do so only because they're surrounded by a professional staff that can supply technical expertise.
- A representative body chosen by lot would not stand alone. It could invite experts, rely on professionals to moderate debates and put questions to citizens. Moreover, it could be given time to learn the ropes and secretarial staff to prepare documents.

- Because citizens chosen by lot do not have to bother with party activities, campaigning or media appearances, they will have more time than their elected colleagues in the other legislative chamber. They can devote themselves full time to their legislative work: studying dossiers, listening to experts, discussing among themselves.

- Everyone contributes according to his or her talents and ambitions. Those who think themselves able to take on demanding governmental work can put their names down for the Agenda Council, the Review Panels, the Rules Council and the Oversight Council while those who have concrete ideas for specific legislation are welcome on an Interest Panel. Those who prefer to take things easy can wait to see if they are called to join the Policy Jury for one or two days, which is like going to vote when you don't follow politics daily.

- Juries for criminal trials that are chosen by lot prove that people generally take their task extremely seriously. The fear of a chamber that behaves recklessly or irresponsibly is unfounded. If we agree that twelve people can decide in good faith about the freedom or imprisonment of a fellow citizen, then we can be confident that a multiple of them can and will serve the interests of the community in a responsible manner.

- All experiments with citizens' forums show that, in general, the behaviour of participants chosen by lot is dedicated and constructive and their recommendations surprisingly sophisticated. Of course this does not mean everything will be perfect, but elected representatives have their weaknesses too and sometimes their laws are not thought through.

• Why do we accept the fact that lobbies, think tanks and all kinds of interest groups can influence policy yet hesitate to give a say to ordinary citizens, who are after all what it's all about?

• Moreover, a chamber of representatives chosen by lot would not stand alone. In this phase of democracy, legislation would arise from the interaction between it and an elected chamber. Idiots in power, if you insist, but not as absolute rulers.

Anyone who looks something up on Google Maps these days will find there's a choice between a map and a satellite image, one better for planning the route, the other for looking at the surroundings. Democracy is just like that. The representation of the people is a map of society, a simplified representation of a complex reality, and because that representation is used to make a rough sketch of the future (and what is politics about if not making a rough sketch of the future?), this map needs to be as detailed as possible, so that topographical map and aerial photograph complement each other. We urgently need to move towards a bi-representative model, a system of representation that is brought about both through voting and by drawing lots. After all, both have their good points, the expertise of professional politicians and the freedom of citizens who do not need re-election. The electoral and aleatoric models therefore go hand in hand.

The bi-representative system is at this point the best remedy for the Democratic Fatigue Syndrome from which so many countries are suffering. Mutual distrust between rulers and ruled will be reduced if their roles are no longer so clearly separated. Citizens who gain access to the governmental level through the drawing of lots will discover the complexity of political dealings, a marvellous training in democracy. Politicians in turn will discover an aspect of the civilian population that they generally underestimate, a capacity for rational, constructive decision-making. They will discover that some laws are accepted more quickly if ordinary people are involved from the beginning, more support making decisive action possible. In short, the bi-representative model is relational therapy for rulers and ruled.

Perhaps this dual system will eventually have to give way to a fully allotted system (Bouricius' phase 5); after all, democracy is an ongoing process. But at this point the combination of sortition and election is the most effective cure available as it takes what is best about the populist tradition (the desire for more authentic representation) without the dangerous illusion of a monolithic people. It incorporates the best of technocratic tradition (valuing the technical expertise of non-elected professionals) without giving experts the final word, and it also makes use of the best of the tradition of direct democracy (the horizontal culture of participatory consultation) without its anti-parliamentarianism. Finally, it reassesses the best aspects of classic representative democracy (the importance of delegation in making government possible) without the electoral fetishism that always goes along with it. Through this combination of beneficial elements, legitimacy grows and efficiency increases as the more the governed identify with the government, the more those in power can govern decisively. The bi-representative model will steer democracy into calmer waters.

When should the transition start? Now. Where? In Europe. Why? The European Union has an advantage. What? It offers shelter to member states that have the courage to innovate in ways that affect their democratic foundations.

Governmental renovation is always a perilous undertaking. At a local level, cities and municipal councils started to work with citizen participation on a large scale only after being encouraged to do so by their national governments. In its turn, the European Union could think of measures that would stimulate and encourage member states to set up useful pilot projects. After all, the Union was the first to try out random sampling and deliberative democracy on a large scale.[122] It was also the Union that chose to name 2013 the Year of the Citizen. What are the high democratic ideals of the Union worth if democracy is crumbling in so many of its member states?

The crisis in the southern member states (Greece, Italy, Spain, Portugal and Cyprus) has brought the spectre of a post-democracy closer, while in Hungary and Greece crypto-fascist movements have been more than merely crypto for some time. In Italy and Greece, technocrats have taken over from democratic governments for short periods. In the Netherlands, France and the United Kingdom populism has become a major factor, and in the recent past, Belgium spent a year and a half without a government. And so on.

It would be interesting to try out the bi-representative model for the first time in a country like Belgium. No other member of the European Union has experienced so acutely the symptoms of Democratic Fatigue Syndrome. After the election of 2010, 541 days passed before a governmental team emerged, an absolute world record. Moreover, no other country today offers such a great opportunity to successfully implement sortition. From 2014 onwards, Belgium will no longer have a directly elected Senate. At the federal level, legislative power will henceforth lie exclusively with the parliament, the Chamber of Representatives. Over past decades much national power has been transferred to lower governmental strata: Flanders, Wallonia, Brussels and the German-speaking region.[123] To keep the different levels formally in contact with each other, the Senate is now evolving into a chamber of reflection, a meeting place for the various regional powers in the country. The Senate was once a space for the Belgian aristocracy, like the British House of Lords, but now it is more a chamber for regional diversity, like the American Senate. Fifty of the sixty senators have their origins in regional parliaments, the other ten are co-opted. The proportion of elected senators has been reduced systematically. In 1830 the entire Senate was directly elected but today none of its members are elected, which fact opens up opportunities for sortition. Successive changes to the constitution have made the population familiar with the idea that direct elections are no longer an absolute precondition for putting together the national assemblies. If there is one place in the European Union where aleatoric-representative democracy has a chance of being introduced, then it is in the recently reformed Belgian Senate.[124]

In a bi-representative Belgium, the Senate could consist purely of citizens chosen by lot, while the lower house could continue to accommodate elected citizens. How many senators there should be, how lots should be drawn, what powers such a Senate should have, how long its mandate should last and what remuneration would be reasonable are not questions to answer now. It is more important to think about the gradual introduction of multi-body sortition. With the support of the EU, the national government could first apply sortition to the making of a single law (for example to determine what powers would be retained by the federal state). This would require only a few Interest Panels, a Review Panel, a Citizen Jury, and politicians could decide beforehand what was to be done with the result. Would the advice be binding or non-binding and when would it be given the force of law?

If experiences were to be positive, the use of sortition could be expanded to a specific policy domain, preferably one that is too delicate to be resolved by party politics (Bouricius' phase 2). In Ireland the Convention on the Constitution looked at gay marriage, women's rights, blasphemy and electoral law. In Belgium it might be a matter of the environment, asylum and migration, and issues concerning the different linguistic communities. To achieve this it would be necessary to organise an Agenda Council, a Rules Council and an Oversight Council, making citizen consultation a permanent part of the governmental archipelago, the complex of islands that communicate with each other in a new democracy to give shape to the whole.[125] In a subsequent phase, politicians would decide whether or not to make citizen participation through sortition permanent and follow up with the necessary arrangements – the Senate could be converted into a legislative organ consisting of a number of different bodies (Bouricius' phase 4).

Belgium could become the first country in Europe to introduce the bi-representative system in practice. Just as Iceland and Ireland have boldly seized upon the financial-economic crisis of recent years as an opportunity to crowdsource their constitutions, Belgium could seize upon its political crisis of recent years to rejuvenate its democracy. There are other countries too where a pilot phase would seem appropriate, for example Portugal, because of the crisis but also because of its familiarity with participative budgets in what is, all things considered, still a young democracy; Estonia, an even younger democracy that faces a huge problem in the form of the need to decide on the part to be played by the Russian minority; Croatia, the youngest member of the European Union, where active citizenship and good governance are now being actively promoted; the Netherlands, with its experience of an Electoral System Citizens Forum and its long tradition of consultation, and so on. It seems to me in any case sensible to start with relatively small member states.

This proposal is not as futuristic as it may appear at first sight. Citizens chosen by lot already have power and, in a few years from now, opinion polls that use random sampling will have evolved all over Europe from neutral barometers of the political climate into extremely important instruments for allowing political parties to adjust their messages. They do not merely measure the popularity of this or that party, politician or measure. They are becoming political facts in their own right and wield a huge amount of influence, as governments attribute great value to them and decision-makers take account of them. The aim of those who propose sortition is to do no more than to make transparent a process that already exists.

In short, what are we waiting for?

Conclusion

OUR DEMOCRACY IS being wrecked by being limited
to elections, even though elections weren't invented as
a democratic instrument. That, in one sentence, is the
argument I develop in the first three chapters of this
essay, while in the fourth chapter I examine the case for
the reintroduction of a far more democratic instrument
historically, sortition.

But what if nothing changes? What if national
governments, parties and politicians decide that drawing
lots is all well and good, but that they have already done
a great deal for the citizen in recent years and thought up
countless new instruments? Which is true. In more and
more countries, anyone with reason to complain can go to
an ombudsman, anyone who has an opinion can vote in
a referendum from time to time and anyone who collects
enough signatures can put an issue on the agenda as a
citizens' initiative. These are forms of participation that
didn't exist a few years ago, when a government would
usually only enter into dialogue with unions, councils,
commissions and itself.

The new instruments are valuable, especially now
that organised civil society has less of a say, but they

still fall far short of what's needed. Citizens' initiatives bring the needs of the people to the doorstep of the legislator, as if they were bottles of milk, and no further. In a referendum people must wait until they can pick a ready-made piece of legislation out of those on offer, and only then can they, in a mad frenzy, throw themselves on their favoured option. Conversations with the ombudsman take place in the garden, as it were, a good distance from the legislative process. No closer. (The ombudsman might be described as the government's gardener, sometimes chatting with the neighbours and listening to their concerns.)

New instruments certainly, but they still function as desperate ways of keeping the citizen out. The doors and windows of the legislative house remain closed and no one gets in, not even through the cat flap. However, in the light of the economic crisis this degree of agoraphobia should act as a wake-up call. It's as if politics has shut itself up in its own castle and is peering out from behind the curtains at the uproar on the street, an unhelpful attitude which only increases the citizen's feeling of distrust and causes further unrest.

Without drastic adjustment, this system cannot last much longer. If you look at the decline in voter turnout and party membership, and at the way politicians are held in contempt, if you look at how difficult it is to form governments, how little they can do and how harshly they are punished for it, if you look at how quickly populism, technocracy and anti-parliamentarianism are rising, if you look at how more and more citizens are longing for participation and how quickly that desire can tip over into frustration, then you realise we are up to our necks. There isn't much time left.

It's very simple: either politics throws open the doors or it won't be long before they'll be kicked in by angry citizens shouting slogans like 'No taxation without participation!' as they smash every last stick of furniture and walk out with the chandelier of power.

This is alas no fantasy. While I was working on this book, Transparency International published its latest 'Global Corruption Barometer' and the findings are downright shocking. Political parties everywhere are regarded as the most corrupt organisations on earth. In practically all Western democracies they come in at number one while in the European Union the figures are nothing less than tragic.

How long can this go on? It's an untenable situation and if I were a politician I'd be losing sleep. As a passionate democrat, I already am. This is a time bomb. We may seem to be in a quiet period, but it's the calm before the storm, the calm of 1850, when the issue of workers' rights seemed to have died down. But the issue was still smouldering, the explosion was yet to come and that was the calm before a long period of great instability. In those days it was all about the right to vote, now it's all about the right to speak, but in essence it's the same battle, the battle for political emancipation and for democratic participation. We must decolonise democracy. We must democratise democracy.

Once again: what are we waiting for?

Acknowledgements

THE IDEA FOR this book came to fruition when I was walking the Pyrenees from west to east in the summer of 2012. Stranded in the French-Basque village of Aldudes by persistent fog, I came upon a copy of *The Social Contract* by Jean-Jacques Rousseau in an old school building. The passage about drawing lots had such an effect on me that I copied it into my diary and for weeks I went round with it lodged in my brain, building the basic structure of the essay in my head, during long climbs in the high mountains. Yet this book is more than the daydream of a solitary walker. It's the result of several years of reading, travelling and listening.

Without the experience of the G1000 I would never have started writing the book. When I decided in February 2011 to initiate a wide-ranging project to increase citizen participation in Belgium I had no idea it would be such an intense undertaking or that it would teach me so much. I owe a great debt of thanks to the extraordinarily inspiring team behind the organisation. We barely knew each other, if at all, beforehand, but I invariably experienced the group as warm, intelligent and dedicated. It was columnist Paul Hermant who first drew my attention to sortition.

Constitutional specialist Sébastien Van Drooghenbroeck spoke with me at the very first meeting about the work of Bernard Manin. Our methodologists Min Reuchamps and Didier Caluwaerts had just completed their doctorates on deliberative democracy and they told me about the experiments carried out by James Fishkin. Our campaign organiser Cato Léonard was from the telecoms sector and during countless car trips to and from fundraising events she drew my attention to the growing importance of 'co-creation' and stakeholder management in business life. I cherish the memories of all those avid, enthusiastic conversations. I also had a great time talking with Benoît Derenne. He became G1000's spokesman on the French-language side as I was on the Flemish side. Having set up the Foundation for Future Generations, he had a great deal of practical experience in organising citizen participation at a regional and European level, and as a Swiss Belgian he often had refreshing ideas about democracy, such as the time when, during a meeting, he asked himself out loud why some members of the Senate could not simply be chosen by drawing lots.

Within the G1000 I would also like to thank Peter Vermeersch, Dirk Jacobs, Dave Sinardet, Francesca Vanthielen, Miriana Frattarola, Fatma Girretz, Myriam Stoffen, Jonathan Van Parys and Fatima Zibouh: not only great interlocutors but good friends. Aline Goethals, Ronny David, François Xavier Lefebvre and many others joined them along the way and are now helping to carry the load. This is not the place to thank the project's hundreds of volunteers, thousands of donors and more than twelve thousand sympathisers, but I would especially like to mention all the participants in the citizens' summit of 2011 and the citizens' panel of 2012. More than anything they convinced me that citizens can and will collaborate to build the future of democracy.

This book began to take shape when I had the honour of occupying the Cleveringa chair at the University of Leiden in the academic year 2011–12, an honorary professorship established to reflect on law, freedom and responsibility in the spirit of the great, courageous law professor Rudolph Cleveringa, who in 1940 spoke out against the dismissal of Jewish colleagues. The title of my inaugural lecture was 'Democracy gasping for breath: the dangers of electoral fundamentalism'. I would like to thank the College of Deacons, and especially the late Willem Willems, former deacon of the Faculty of Archaeology, and former rector Paul van der Heijden, for their faith in me. Thanks also to all the students of the honours college for the investigative seminars on elections and democratisation in non-Western countries such as Afghanistan. Belgian academics including Philippe Van Parijs, Chantal Mouffe, Min Reuchamps and Paul De Grauwe offered me the chance to talk about my ideas. Two leading ancient historians, Mogens Herman Hansen from Copenhagen and Paul Cartledge from Cambridge, very generously shared their views on sortition in ancient Greece. I am sincerely grateful to all of them.

On trips abroad I had the privilege of meeting countless political scientists and democracy activists. In the Netherlands I learned a great deal from Josien Pieterse, Yvonne Zonderop and Willem Schinkel. In Germany Carsten Berg and Martin Wilhelm made a great impression and the same goes for Carl Henrik Frederiksson in Austria, Inga Wachsmann and Pierre Calame in France, Igor Štiks and Srećko Horvat in Croatia, and Bernice Chauly and A. Samad Said in Malaysia. The latter is a national icon, a legendary poet-dissident who at the age of eighty continues indefatigably to fight for democracy.

I do not belong in the category of citizens who despise politicians by definition. In fact I found it instructive to listen closely to what people like Sabine de Bethune, former president of the Belgian Senate, and Gerdi Verbeet, former president of the Dutch Lower House, told me from the perspective of hands-on politics. In preparation for writing this book I had long conversations with several veterans of Belgian politics. Sven Gatz, Inge Vervotte, Caroline Gennez, Jos Geysels and Hugo Coveliers were particularly generous in sharing their experiences. I have not quoted them directly – the book goes beyond the Belgian context – but what they told me enriched my outlook, so many thanks to all of them.

Various people answered my questions: Marc Swyngedouw, Marnix Beyen, Walter Van Steenbrugge, Filip De Rynck, Jelle Haemers, Fabien Moreau, Thomas Saalfeld and Sona N. Golder. With Kenneth Carter I was able to exchange ideas about the British Columbia Citizens' Assembly on Electoral Reform, for which he was chief researcher. No less fascinating was the contact I had with Eiríkur Bergmann and Jane Suiter, who were closely involved with the constitutional councils in Iceland and Ireland. I would particularly like to thank Terry Bouricius and David Schecter from the US for a lively and ongoing exchange about their multi-body sortition model. The same goes out to Iain Walker and Janette Hartz-Karp for their fantastic and innovative work in Australia.

Peter Vermeersch, Emmy Deschuttere and Luc Huyse read the text and pleased me greatly, as always, with their discerning comments. I'd be nowhere without their friendship. Charlotte Bonduel helped me with online research and the compilation of a number of figures and it was a pleasure to work with her. Wil Hansen was once again my magnificent editor and it was he who one fine day in my studio suggested the title. He thought of *Against Interpretation* by Susan Sontag, I of *Against Method* by Paul Feyerabend, and together we savoured the words.

Brussels, July 2013

Bibliography

THE MOST IMPORTANT book I read for this essay was *The Principles of Representative Government* by Bernard Manin (Cambridge, 1997). It was followed by several other excellent works. British political thinker Oliver Dowlen wrote *The Political Potential of Sortition: A Study of the Random Selection of Citizens for Public Office* (Exeter, 2009), German professor of political theory and the history of ideas Hubertus Buchstein published *Demokratie und Lotterie: Das Los als politisches Entscheidungsinstrument von Antike bis zur EU* (Frankfurt, 2009), Parisian political scientist Yves Sintomer was responsible for *Petite histoire de l'expérimentation démocratique: Tirage au sort et politique d'Athènes à nos jours* (Paris, 2011), and from Canadian professor of political science Francis Dupuis-Déri came *Démocratie: Histoire politique d'un mot aux États-Unis et en France* (Montreal, 2013).

Those seeking a more general history of what has befallen democracy will learn a good deal from *The Life and Death of Democracy* by John Keane (London, 2009). More technical, but extremely impressive, are the studies by Pierre Rosanvallon: *Counter-Democracy: Politics in an Age of Distrust* (New York, 2008), *Democratic Legitimacy:*

Impartiality, Reflexivity, Proximity (Princeton, 2011) and *The Society of Equals* (Cambridge, MA, 2011). The two best books on democracy in Classical Antiquity are Mogens Herman Hansen's *The Athenian Democracy in the Age of Demosthenes* (London, 1999) and Paul Cartledge's *Democracy: A Life* (Oxford, 2016). Sound, factual information about the current system can be found in the excellent reference work *Representative Government in Modern Europe* by Michael Gallagher, Michael Laver and Peter Mair (London, 2011). By Mair, the Irish political scientist, who died far too young, a posthumous collection has been published called *Ruling the Void: The Hollowing of Western Democracy* (London, 2013). His essays influenced me greatly in writing Chapter 1.

Arguments in favour of sortition have been looked at and discussed openly in recent years in academic circles. Barbara Goodwin, professor of politics at the University of East Anglia, published the influential *Justice by Lottery* well over twenty years ago (Chicago, 1992), placing the essential value of sortition in democracy back on the agenda. Lyn Carson and Brian Martin, two researchers from Australia, wrote *Random Selection in Politics* (Westport, 1999). Lately research has accelerated and Oliver Dowlen, whose *Political Potential of Sortition* I mention above, is one of the founders of the Society for Democracy Including Random Selection. Along with Gil Delannoi he edited the collection *Sortition: Theory and Practice* (Exeter, 2010). He is also the author of the more succinct *Sorted: Civic Lotteries and the Future of Public Participation* (Toronto, 2008), which is available free as a pdf (http://ebookpoint.us/scribd/sorted-civic-lotteries-and-the-future-of-public-participation-11446805). Terrill Bouricius is working on a book with the promising working title *The Trouble with Elections: Everything You Thought You Knew about Democracy is Wrong*.

I found concrete proposals for the reintroduction of sortition in Ernest Callenbach & Michael Phillips, *A Citizen Legislature* (Berkeley, 1985), in Anthony Barnett & Peter Carty, *The Athenian Option: Radical Reform for the House of Lords* (London, 1998), in Keith Sutherland, *A People's Parliament: A (Revised) Blueprint for a Very English Revolution* (Exeter, 2008) and in the abovementioned works by Sintomer and Buchstein. This is merely a selection. A more complete list can be found in Antoine Vergnes' contribution to the collection by Gil Delannoi & Oliver Dowlen, under the title 'A brief survey of the literature of sortition'. My Figure 5 refers to the latest proposals. The article by Terrill Bouricius, 'Democracy through multi-body sortition: Athenian lessons for the modern day', *Journal of Public Deliberation* (2013) 9, 1, article 11 is available online (http://www.publicdeliberation.net/cgi/viewcontent.cgi?article=1220&context=jpd).

The literature on deliberative democracy is extensive. Among works to which I refer are James Fishkin, *When the People Speak: Deliberative Democracy and Public*

Consultation (Oxford, 2009) and a recent French anthology, *La Démocratie délibérative: Anthologie des textes fondamentaux* (Paris, 2010), by Charles Girard and Alice Le Goff. The most recent developments can be followed in academic journals such as *International Journal of Public Participation* and *Journal of Public Deliberation.*

A great deal has been published in recent years on the subject of citizen participation. On the situation in Flanders, Filip De Rynck and Karolien Dezeure published *Burgerparticipatie in Vlaamse steden: Naar een innoverend participatiebeleid* (Bruges, 2009) and on France, Georges Ferreboeuf wrote *Participation citoyenne et ville* (Paris, 2011). Valuable practical advice for local policy can be found in *'Wij gooien het de inspraak in': Een onderzoek naar de uitgangspunten voor behoorlijke burgerparticipatie* by the Dutch National Ombudsman (the Hague, 2009) and in *Beslist anders beslissen: Het surplus voor besturen als bewoners het beleid mee sturen* by Samenlevingsopbouw West-Vlaanderen (Bruges, 2011). The King Baudouin Foundation has published an excellent handbook called *Participatory Methods Toolkit: A Practitioner's Manual* (Brussels, 2003), which is available online as a pdf (http://archive.unu.edu/hq/library/Collection/PDF_files/CRIS/PMT.pdf).

In the Low Countries debate is raging over the future of parliamentary democracy. For Flanders I refer readers to Thomas Decreus, *Een paradijs waait uit de storm: Over markt, democratie en verzet* (Berchem, 2013) and Manu Claeys, *Stilstand: Over machtspolitiek, betweterbestuur en achterkamerdemocratie* (Louvain, 2013). For the Netherlands I think first of all of the work of Willem Schinkel, *De nieuwe democratie: Naar andere vormen van politiek* (Amsterdam, 2012), but also *Polderen 3.0: Nederland en het algemeen belang* by Yvonne Zonderop (Loused, 2012) and *Vertrouwen is goed maar begrijpen is beter: Over de vitaliteit van onze parlementaire democratie* by Gerdi Verbeet (Amsterdam, 2012). The most interesting academic studies are two collections: *Democratie doorgelicht: Het functioneren van de Nederlandse democratie*, compiled by Rudy Andeweg and Jacques Thomassen (Leiden, 2011), and *Omstreden democratie: Over de problemen van een succesverhaal*, compiled by Remieg Aerts and Peter de Goede (Amsterdam, 2013).

Several organisations campaigning for reforms to democracy are particularly active on the internet. The international sites that spring to mind are:

- openDemocracy.net: independent non-profit with often outstanding contributions.
- participedia.net: the most important international site about participatory democracy.
- sortition.net: portal site with historical texts and many useful links.

- equalitybylot.wordpress.com: a rich and varied blog with a lively online community of 'klcroterians' who discuss the subject of sortition.

More and more Western countries have national platforms for democratic innovation, and many of their sites are extremely interesting:

- The Jefferson Centre for New Democratic Processes (USA): the name says enough.
- Center for Deliberative Democracy (USA): housed at Stanford University, where James Fishkin is based, with useful information about deliberative polls.
- AmericaSpeaks and GlobalVoices (USA): organises large-scale citizens' forums; a rich and diverse site.
- newDemocracy.com.au (Australia): plenty of clear information about sortition.
- We the Citizens (Ireland): site of the large-scale citizens' initiative in Ireland.
- 38 Degrees (UK): influential organisation for citizen participation with more than a million members.
- Mehr Demokratie (Germany): twenty-five years old but militant as ever, campaigning for a citizens' right of initiative and for referendums.
- Democracy International (EU): based in Germany, a pan-European organisation that has for years advocated a European Citizens' Initiative.

- Teknologi-rådet (Denmark): Danish Technology Council, which has devised countless participatory processes that are explained in English on its site.
- NetwerkDemocratie (The Netherlands): Dutch platform for governmental reform, including through the use of digital technologies.
- G1000 (Belgium): website in four languages of the citizens' initiative G1000, now part of the Foundation for Future Generations.
- King Baudouin Foundation (Belgium): an internationally valued player, partly for its long-standing project on governance.
- ¡Democracía Real Ya! (Spain): a militant organisation campaigning for democracy that grew out of the popular protests of March 2011.
- Association pour une démocratie directe (France): website of a young, dynamic organisation that campaigns for greater transparency.

Endnotes

1   http://www.worldvaluessurvey.org/WVSOnline.jsp.

2   Eric Hobsbawm, 1995: *Age of Extremes: The Short Twentieth Century, 1914–1991*. London, 112.

3   Freedom House, 2013: *Freedom in the World 2013: Democratic Breakthroughs in the Balance*. London, 28-29.

4   Ronald Inglehart, 2003: 'How solid is mass support for democracy – and how can we measure it?' *Science and Politics*, January, 51-57.

5   In 1999–2000, 33.3% of those questioned said that a strong leader who need take no account of elections or parliament was a good idea. By 2005–08 the figure was 38.1%. As for faith, in 2005–08 52.4% of those questioned had little or no faith in their government, 60.3% in their parliament and 72.8% in the political parties.

6   Eurobarometer, 2012: Standard Eurobarometer 78: First Results. Autumn 2012, 14. http://ec.europa.eu/public_opinion/archives/eb/eb78/eb78_first_en.pdf (last accessed 26 March 2016).

7   http://www.eurofound.europa.eu/surveys/smt/3eqls/index.EF.php. The figures for press, parliament and government are from 2012, those for political parties from 2007.

8   Peter Kanne, 2011: *Gedoogdemocratie: Heeft stemmen eigenlijk wel zin?* Amsterdam, 83.

9   Koen Abts, Marc Swyngedouw & Dirk Jacobs, 2011: 'Politieke betrokkenheid en institutioneel wantrouwen. De spiraal van

het wantrouwen doorbroken?', in Koen Abts et al., *Nieuwe tijden, nieuwe mensen: Belgen over arbeid, gezin, ethiek, religie en politiek.* Louvain, 173-214.

10 Luc Huyse, 1969: *De niet-aanwezige staatsburger.* Antwerp, 154-57.

11 Michael Gallagher, Michael Laver & Peter Mair, 2011: *Representative Government in Modern Europe.* Maidenhead, 306.

12 http://nl.wikipedia.org/wiki/Opkomstplicht (last accessed 26 March 2016).

13 Koenraad De Ceuninck et al., 2013: 'De bolletjeskermis van 14 oktober 2012: politiek is een kaartspel'. *Sampol* 1, 53.

14 Yvonne Zonderop, 2012: 'Hoe het populisme kon aarden in Nederland'. http://yvonnezonderop.nl/wp-content/uploads/2014/01/507_CP_RRadical_Dutch_web.pdf (accessed 28 March 2016), 50.

15 http://www.parlement.com/id/vh8lnhrp8wsz/opkomstpercentage_tweede

16 Michael Gallagher, Michael Laver & Peter Mair, 2011: *Representative Government in Modern Europe.* Maidenhead, 311.

17 Paul F. Whitely, 2011: 'Is the party over? The decline of party activism and membership across the democratic world'. *Party Politics* 16, 1, 21-44.

18 Ingrid Van Biezen, Peter Mair & Thomas Poguntke, 2012: 'Going, going, . . . gone? The decline of party membership in contemporary Europe'. *European Journal of Political Research* 51, 33, 38.

19 http://nl.wikipedia.org/wiki/Historisch_overzicht_van_kabinetsformaties_(Nederland) (last accessed 28 March 2016). See also Sona N. Golder, 2010: 'Bargaining Delays in the Government Formation Process'. *Comparative Political Studies* 43, 1, 3-32.

20   Hanne Marthe Narud & Henry Valen, 2005: 'Coalition membership and electoral performance in Western Europe'. Paper for presentation at the 2005 NOPSA Meeting, Reykjavik, August 11–13, 2005. See also Peter Mair, 2011: 'How Parties Govern', lecture at the Central European University, Budapest, 29 April 2011, http://www.youtube.com/watch?v=mgyjdzfcbps, from 27:50 (last accessed 28 March 2016).

21   Tweede kamer der Staten-Generaal, 2008–09: *Vertrouwen en zelfvertrouwen. Parlementaire zelfreflectie 2007–2009.* 31, 845, nos. 2-3, 38-39.

22   Ibid., 34.

23   Hansje Galesloot, 2005: *Vinden en vasthouden. Werving van politiek en bestuurlijk talent.* Amsterdam.

24   Herman Van Rompuy, 2013: 'Over stilte en leiderschap', speech delivered in Turnhout on 7 June 2013, http://www.destillekempen.be/stiltenieuws/stiltenieuws/88-herman-van-rompuy-over-stilte-en-leiderschap (accessed 28 March 2016).

25   In an earlier essay, *Pleidooi voor populisme* (Amsterdam, 2008), I advocated not less but better populism. After all, populist voting behaviour expresses, in an inconvenient way, the ever-present desire for political involvement among the less educated strata of society.

26   Mark Bovens & Anchrit Wille, 2011: *Diplomademocratie. Over de spanning tussen meritocratie en democratie.* Amsterdam.

27   Cited in Raad voor het Openbaar Bestuur, 2010: *Vertrouwen op democratie.* The Hague, 38.

28   John R. Hibbing & Elizabeth Theiss-Morse, 2002: *Stealth Democracy: Americans' Beliefs about How Government Should Work.* Cambridge, 156.

29   Sarah van Gelder (ed.), 2011: *This Changes Everything: Occupy Wall Street and the 99% Movement.* San Francisco, 18.

30 For an excellent analysis: Tom Vandyck, '"Compromis", een nieuw vuil woord'. *De Morgen*, 11 July 2011, 13.

31 Ibid.

32 Lars Mensel: 'Dissatisfaction makes me hopeful', interview with Michael Hardt. *The European*, 15 April 2013.

33 Lenny Flank (ed.), 2011: *Voices From the 99 Percent: An Oral History of the Occupy Wall Street Movement*. St Petersburg, Florida, 91.

34 Early books about Occupy Wall Street are rather self-glorifying. As well as the collections edited by van Gelder and Flank, I read Todd Gitlin, *Occupy Nation: The Roots, the Spirit and the Promise of Occupy Wall Street* (New York, 2012) and the work of the collective Writers for the 99%, called *Occupying Wall Street: The Inside Story of an Action that Changed America* (New York, 2011).

35 Sarah van Gelder (ed.), 2011: *This Changes Everything: Occupy Wall Street and the 99% Movement*. San Francisco, 25.

36 Mary Kaldor & Sabine Selchow, 2012: 'The "bubbling up" of subterranean politics in Europe'. Report, London School of Economics and Political Science, June 2012, 10 (last accessed online at http://eprints.lse.ac.uk/44873/1/The%20 %E2%80%98bubbling%20up%E2%80%99%20of%20 subterranean%20politics%20in%20Europe(lsero).pdf, 28 March 2016).

37 Ibid., 12.

38 V.I. Lenin, 1917 (1976): *The State and Revolution*, Beijing, 23-24 & 41. Also available at https://www.marxists.org/archive/ lenin/works/1917/staterev/ch03.htm.

39 Chris Hedges & Joe Sacco, 2012: *Days of Destruction, Days of Revolt*. New York, 232.

40 Pierre Rosanvallon, 2012: *Democratie en tegendemocratie*, Amsterdam, 54.

41 Thomas Frank, 2012: 'To the Precinct Station. How theory met practice . . . and drove it absolutely crazy', *The Baffler* no. 21.

42 Willem Schinkel, 2012: *De nieuwe democratie: Naar andere vormen van politiek*. Amsterdam, 168.

43 Stéphane Hessel, 2013: *À nous de jouer: Appel aux indignés de cette Terre*. Paris, 63.

44 Fiona Ehlers et al.: 'Europe's lost generation finds its voice'. *SpiegelOnline*, 13 March 2013.

45 Through its 'liquid feedback' software, for instance, and its notion of 'delegative' democracy.

46 David Van Reybrouck: 'De democratie in ademnood: de gevaren van electoraal fundamentalisme'. Cleveringa lecture, University of Leiden, 28 November 2011.

47 Pierre Rosanvallon, 2008: *Democratic Legitimacy: Impartiality, Reflexivity, Proximity*. Princeton, 21-22, 55-56.

48 Edmund Burke, 1774: 'Speech to the Electors of Bristol'. press-pubs.uchicago.edu/founders/documents/v1ch13s7.html.

49 Jean-Jacques Rousseau 1762 (1947), *The Social Contract*, New York, Book IV, Chapter II (eighteenth-century translation, revised and edited by Charles Frankel), 94.

50 Lars Mensel: 'Dissatisfaction makes me hopeful', interview with Michael Hardt. *The European*, 15 April 2013.

51 Colin Crouch, 2004: *Post-Democracy*. Cambridge, 4.

52 Marc Michils, 2011: *Open boek. Over eerlijke reclame in een transparante wereld*. Louvain, 100-01.

53 Jan de Zutter, 2013: 'Het zijn de burgers die aan het stuur zitten'. Interview with Jan Rotmans. *Sampol* 20, 3, 24.

54 The renewed interest in Athenian democracy can be attributed to the English translation of the life's work of Danish classicist M.H. Hansen: *The Athenian Democracy in the Age of Demosthenes* (Oxford, 1991). The original, a minute analysis of the fourth-century sources, is in six volumes.

55   Bernard Manin, 1995 (1997): *The Principles of Representative Government*. Cambridge, 1, 94, 236.

56   See Bibliography.

57   Aristotle, 350 bc (1885), *Politics,* Oxford, vol. 1, book four, part IX & book six, part II (translated by Benjamin Jowett), 124, 125, 189.

58   Terrill Bouricius, 2013: 'Democracy through multi-body sortition: Athenian lessons for the modern day'. *Journal of Public Deliberation* 9, 1, article 11.

59   Miranda Mowbray & Dieter Gollman, 2007: 'Electing the Doge of Venice: analysis of a 13th century protocol'. www.hpl. hp.com/techreports/2007/HPL-2007-28R1.pdf (last accessed 29 March 2016).

60   Yves Sintomer, 2011: *Petite histoire de l'expérimentaion démocratique*: *Tirage au sort et politique d'Athènes à nos jours*. Paris, 86.

61   Hubertus Buchstein, 2009: *Demokratie und Lotterie: Das Lot als politisches: Entscheidungsinstrument von Antike bis zur EU*. Frankfurt, 186.

62   Montesquieu, 1748 (1989), *The Spirit of the Laws*, Cambridge, book II, chapter II (translated by Anne M. Cohler, Basia Carolyn Miller & Harold Samuel Stone), 13-14.

63   Jean-Jacques Rousseau 1762 (1947), *The Social Contract*, New York, book IV, chapter III (eighteenth-century translation, revised and edited by Charles Frankel), 97-98.

64   Bernard Manin, 1995 (1997): *The Principles of Representative Government*. Cambridge, 79.

65   Montesquieu, 1748 (1989), *The Spirit of the Laws*, Cambridge, book II, chapter II (translated by Anne M. Cohler, Basia Carolyn Miller & Harold Samuel Stone), 10.

66   John Adams, 1851: *The Works of John Adams*. Boston, vol. 6, 484.

67 James Madison, 1787: *Federalist Paper no. 10*. http://press-pubs.uchicago.edu/founders/documents/v1ch4s19.html (last accessed 29 March 2016).

68 Cited in Francis Dupuis-Déri, 2013: *Démocratie: Histoire politique d'un mot aux États-Unis et en France*. Montreal, 138.

69 Ibid., 149.

70 Howard Zinn, 1999 (2015): *A People's History of the United States*. New York, 90.

71 Francis Dupuis-Déri, 2013: *Démocratie: Histoire politique d'un mot aux États-Unis et en France*. Montreal, 87.

72 For a thorough analysis, see Howard Zinn, *A People's History of the United States* (New York, 2005) and Francis Dupuis-Déri, *Démocratie: Histoire politique d'un mot aux États-Unis et en France* (Montreal, 2013).

73 James Madison, 1788: *Federalist Paper no. 57*. http://press-pubs.uchicago.edu/founders/documents/a1_2_3s16.html (accessed 29 March 2016).

74 Bernard Manin, 1995 (1997): *The Principles of Representative Government*. Cambridge, 116-17.

75 Cited in Francis Dupuis-Déri, 2013: *Démocratie: Histoire politique d'un mot aux États-Unis et en France*. Montreal, 155. English original available at http://press-pubs.uchicago.edu/founders/print_documents/v1ch15s61.html

76 Cited in Keith Michael Baker, 1990: *Inventing the French Revolution*. Cambridge, 249.

77 Francis Dupuis-Déri, 2013: *Démocratie: Histoire politique d'un mot aux États-Unis et en France*. Montreal, 112.

78 Edmund Burke, 1790: *Reflections on the Revolution in France*. www.constitution.org/eb/rev_fran.htm (last accessed 29 March 2016).

79   Cited in Andrew Jainchill, 2008, *Reimagining Politics After the Terror: The Republican Origins of French Liberalism*. New York, 43.

80   Cited in Francis Dupuis-Déri, 2013: *Démocratie: Histoire politique d'un mot aux États-Unis et en France*. Montreal. 156.

81   Cited in Yves Sintomer, 2011: *Petite histoire de l'expérimentation démocratique: Tirage au sort et politique d'Athènes à nos jours*. Paris, 120.

82   Alexis de Tocqueville, 1835 & 1840 (1899): *Democracy in America*. New York, book I, part I, chapter VIII (translated by Henry Reeve), 95, 97, 100.

83   Ibid., 226, 228, 229.

84   I make use of E.H. Kossmann, *The Low Countries 1780–1940* (Oxford, 1978), Marc Reynebeau, *Een geschiedenis van België* (Tielt, 2003), Rolf Falter, *1830: De scheiding van Nederland, België en Luxemburg* (Tielt, 2005), Els Witte, Jean-Pierre Nandrin, Eliane Gubin & Gita Deneckere, *Nieuwe geschiedenis van België, deel 1: 1830* (Tielt, 2005) and Els Witte, Jan Craeybeckx & Alain Meynen, *Politieke geschiedenis van België: van 1830 tot heden* (Antwerp, 2005).

85   Rolf Falter, 2005: *1830: De scheiding van Nederland, België en Luxemburg*. Tielt, 203.

86   E.H. Kossmann, 1978, *The Low Countries 1780–1940*. Oxford, 157.

87   John Gilissen, 1968: 'La Constitution belge de 1831: ses sources, son influence'. *Res Publica*, 107-41. See also: P. Lauvaux, 2010: 'La Constitution belge aux sources de la Constitution de Tirnovo', in *L'union fait la force: Étude comparée de la Constitution belge et de la Constitution bulgare*. Brussels, 43-54, and Asem Khalil, 2003: *Which Constitution for the Palestinian Legal System?* Rome, 11.

88 Zachary Elkins, 2010: 'Diffusion and the constitutionalization of Europe'. *Comparative Political Studies* 43, 8/9, 988.

89 J.A. Hawgood, 1960: 'Liberalism and constitutional developments', in *The New Cambridge Modern History, vol. x, The Zenith of European Power, 1830–70*. Cambridge, 191.

90 Hendrik Conscience, 1850: *De loteling*. Antwerp.

91 James W. Headlam, 1891: *Election by Lot at Athens*. Cambridge, 1.

92 Francis Fukuyama, 1992: *The End of History and the Last Man*. New York, 43.

93 David Holmstrom, 1995: 'New kind of poll aims to create an "authentic public voice"'. *The Christian Science Monitor*, 31 August 1995, and James S. Fishkin & Robert C. Luskin, 2005: 'Experimenting with a democratic ideal: deliberative polling and public opinion'. *Acta Politica*, 40, 287.

94 Daniel M. Merkle, 1996: 'The National Issues Convention deliberative poll'. *Public Opinion Quarterly*, 60, 588-619.

95 John Gastil, 1996: *Deliberation at the National Issues Convention: An Observer's Notes*. Albuquerque, 21.

96 David Holmstrom, 1995: 'New kind of poll aims to create an "authentic public voice"'. *The Christian Science Monitor*, 31 August 1995.

97 In Canada, Australia, Northern Ireland, Denmark, Italy, Hungary, Bulgaria, Greece, Poland and for the EU, but also in Brazil, Argentina, Japan, Korea, Macao, Hong Kong and even China. See http://cdd.stanford.edu/.

98 Jeanette Hartz-Karp & Lyn Carson, 2009: 'Putting the people into politics: the Australian Citizens' Parliament'. *International Journal of Public Participation* 3, 1, 18.

99 Manon Sabine de Jongh, 2013: *Group Dynamics in the Citizens' Assembly on Electoral Reform*. PhD thesis, Utrecht, 53.

100 I derive this idea from a conversation with Kenneth Carty, the research director of the citizens' forum in British Columbia, Louvain, 13 December 2012.

101 Manon Sabine de Jongh, 2013: *Group Dynamics in the Citizens' Assembly on Electoral Reform*. PhD thesis, Utrecht, 53-55.

102 Lawrence LeDuc, 2011: 'Electoral reform and direct democracy in Canada: when citizens become involved'. *West European Politics* 34, 3, 559.

103 Ibid., 563.

104 John Parkinson, 2005: 'Rickety bridges: using the media in deliberative democracy'. *British Journal of Political Science* 36, 175-83.

105 Eiríkur Bergmann, 2013: 'Reconstituting Iceland: constitutional reform caught in a new critical order in the wake of crisis'. Conference paper, Leiden, January 2013.

106 http://en.wikipedia.org/wiki/Icelandic_Constitutional_ Assembly_election,_2010 (last accessed 1 April 2016).

107 https://www.washingtonpost.com/blogs/monkey-cage/ wp/2015/06/05/the-irish-vote-for-marriage-equality-started-at- a-constitutional-convention/

108 *De Standaard*, 29 December 2012.

109 Antoine Vergne, 2010: 'A brief survey of the literature of sortition: is the age of sortition upon us?', in Gil Delannoi & Oliver Dowlen (eds), *Sortition: Theory and Practice*. Exeter and Charlottesville, 80. Vergne counts sixteen, but recently several have been added.

110 For the US: Ernest Callenbach & Michael Phillips, *A Citizen Legislature* (Berkeley, 1985; new edition Exeter and Charlottesville, 2008); John Burnheim, *Is Democracy Possible? The Alternative to Electoral Politics* (London, 1985, full text online at http://setis.library.usyd.edu.au/democracy/index.

html, accessed 1 April 2016); Ethan J. Leib, *Deliberative Democracy in America: A Proposal for a Popular Branch of Government* (Philadelphia, 2005); and Kevin O'Leary, *Saving Democracy: A Plan for Real Presentation in America* (Stanford, 2006). For Britain: Anthony Barnett & Peter Carty, *The Athenian Option: Radical Reform for the House of Lords* (London, 1998; new edition 2008, Exeter and Charlottesville); Alex Zakaras, 'Lot and democratic representation: a modest proposal', *Constellations* (2010) 17, 3; Keith Sutherland, *A People's Parliament: A (Revised) Blueprint for a Very English Revolution* (Exeter and Charlottesville, 2008) and Keith Sutherland, 'What sortition can and cannot do' (2011, http://ssrn.com/abstract=1928927, last accessed 1 April 2016). For France: Yves Sintomer, *Petite histoire de l'expérimentation démocratique: Tirage au sort et politique d'Athènes à nos jours* (Paris, 2011). And for the EU: Hubertus Buchstein, *Demokratie und Lotterie: Das Los als politisches Entscheidungsinstrument von Antike bis zur EU* (Frankfurt and New York, 2009) and Hubert Buchstein & Michael Hein, 'Randomizing Europe: the lottery as a political instrument for a reformed European Union', in Gil Delannoi & Oliver Dowlen (eds), *Sortition: Theory and Practice* (Exeter and Charlottesville, 2011), 119-55.

111 Ernest Callenbach & Michael Phillips, 1985 (2008): *A Citizen Legislature*, Exeter, 67.

112 Another difference between this and the proposal by Callenbach and Phillips is that among the six hundred members of the House of Peers would be several representatives of the political parties. They would not be chosen by lot but appointed to form a bridge between the citizens' forum and political parties, rather in the way they did in the Irish constitutional convention. Barnett and Carty followed their American colleagues in suggesting that in sortition the conditions should

be as attractive as possible (substantial salary; compensation to employers) so as to maximise diversity, but believed no one should be forced to participate as they are in some countries with military service or jury service.

113 Anthony Barnett & Peter Carty, 1998 (2008): *The Athenian Option: Radical Reform for the House of Lords*. Exeter, 22.

114 Keith Sutherland, 2011: 'What sortition can and cannot do'. http://ssrn.com/abstract=1928927. See also Keith Sutherland, 2008: *A People's Parliament: A (Revised) Blueprint for a Very English Revolution*. Exeter.

115 Yves Sintomer, 2011: *Petite histoire de l'expérimentation démocratique: Tirage au sort et politique d'Athènes à nos jours*. Paris, 235.

116 Hubertus Buchstein, 2009: *Demokratie und Lotterie: Das Lot als politisches Entscheidungsinstrument von Antike bis zur EU*. Frankfurt, 448.

117 Terrill Bouricius, 2013: 'Democracy through multi-body sortition: Athenian lessons for the modern day'. *Journal of Public Deliberation* 9, 1, article 11, 5.

118 Terrill Bouricius, Email, 14 June 2013.

119 Terrill Bouricius & David Schecter, 2013: 'An idealized design for the legislative branch of government'. *Systems Thinking World Journal* 2, 1.

120 John Keane, 2010: *The Life and Death of Democracy*. London, 737.

121 Alex Guerrero (in preparation): *The Lottocratic Alternative*. Unpublished manuscript.

122 Meeting of the Minds in 2005, European Citizens' Consultations in 2007 and 2009.

123 This is really a matter of three communities (the Flemish, French-language and German-language) and three regions (Flanders, Brussels and Wallonia). Brussels is officially

bilingual in French and Dutch; Wallonia is mainly French-speaking, with a German-speaking area in the east.

124 Secondary reasons are: 1) as a small country it is a suitable place to try out sortition (manageable travel distances, centrality of the capital, proximity to supervisory European institutions); 2) the official use of three languages and the existence of a thoroughly multilingual capital city present considerable challenges to those working with what academics call 'deliberative democracy in divided societies'; 3) the country has a tradition of political innovation, not only with the constitution of 1831 but with the genocide law, the law on gay marriage and its euthanasia legislation, with which it was more than a decade ahead of many other European member states; 4) the complex composition of the population has created the constitutional equivalent of high technology, such as the principle of 'the weighted majority', which has since been taken over at a European level; 5) legally and constitutionally the country has always been a laboratory for the rest of Europe; 6) government and population are increasingly familiar with innovative citizen participation, through the work of a strong civil society (unions, employers' organisations, youth movements, women's movements, family organisations, clubs and societies), through the work of various foundations and institutions (King Baudouin Foundation, Foundation for Future Generations, G1000, Netwerk Participatie, Vlaams Instituut Samenleving en Technologie, States General, Ademloos, De Wakkere Burger, Kwadraet), through countless forms of successful citizen participation (at local, provincial and regional levels): in Belgium, democratic innovation is no longer taboo.

125 John Keane, 2010: *The Life and Death of Democracy*. London, 695-98.

Index

A

absenteeism, voter, 7–8, 16, 164
absolutism, 5, 42, 43
Adams, Gerry, 129
Adams, John, 81, 83–5
adversary democracy, 107
Afghanistan, 39
Afsluitdijk, Netherlands, 12
Agenda Council, 141, 142, 144, 155, 161
agoraphobia, political, 89, 164
aleatoric-representative democracy,
    67, 77, 93, 135, 157, 160; *see also*
    sortition
d'Alembert, Jean, 76
Alexander the Great, 58
American Airlines, 110
American Revolution (1776–89), 41, 43,
    46, 55, 62, 63, 78–88, 93–8, 148
Amsterdam, Netherlands, 12
An Coinbhinsiún ar an mBunreacht, 118
anarchy, 5
d'Anglas, Boissy, 91
Anonymous, 29
anti-parliamentarianism, 30–4, 35, 36, 45,
    48, 54, 158, 165
Antwerp, Belgium, 7, 12
apathy, 4, 5
Arab Spring (2011), 2, 27
Aragon, Kingdom of (1035–1706), 69,
    73–4
aristocracy, 5, 43, 63, 72, 75, 76, 78–105,
    148, 152, 160, 163
Aristotle, 66, 75, 85, 97, 148
Articles of Confederation (1777), 84
Assemblée Nationale, France, 81, 136

Athens, 26, 28, 58–67, 68, 72, 73, 74,
    75–7, 79, 84, 85, 87, 90, 103, 108,
    109, 139–40, 144, 145, 148, 150
Atlantic Monthly, The, 106, 108
austerity, 29
Austin, Texas, 110
Australia, 115
Austria, 8, 9, 18, 99

B

Balkenende, Jan Peter, 122
ballotta, 68, 70–2
banking crises, 12, 28
Barber, Benjamin, 107
Barcelona, Catalonia, 74
Barnave, Antoine, 81
Barnett, Anthony, 135
Belgium, 7, 8, 9, 10, 29, 48, 98–103, 131,
    159–62
Ben Ali, Zine El Abidine, 53
Berlin Wall, 2, 58–9, 61
Berlusconi, Silvio, 17, 23, 51
Beurs van Berlage, Amsterdam, 28
Beyond Adversary Democracy
    (Mansbridge), 107
bi-representative democracy, 150–62
Björk, 128
Bologna, Italy, 70, 73
bottom-up systems, 57, 125
bourgeoisie, 31–2, 46–7, 80, 88, 91
Bouricius, Terrill, 138–50, 155, 157, 161
Bowling Green Park, New York City, 24–6
Brazil, 112, 113
Brescia, Italy, 73
Britain, *see under* United Kingdom

British Columbia, Canada, 117, 118, 119, 121, 122, 149
Brussels, Belgium, 31, 159
Buchstein, Hubertus, 137–8
Bulgaria, 101, 112
Burke, Edmund, 46–7, 89–91
Bush, George Herbert Walker, 106

C
Cairo, Egypt, 27
Callenbach, Ernest, 133–5
Cambridge University, 103
Canada, 81, 115, 117, 119–23, 126, 149, 150
Carty, Peter, 135
Castile, Kingdom of (1230–1516), 74
Catalonia, 123
central banks, 22–3, 28
Chamber of Representatives, Belgium, 159
Channel 4 (UK), 125
Channel Tunnel, 12
China, 23, 25–6, 112, 113
Citizen Juries, 113, 161
citizen participation, 106–31, 149–62, 163–4
Citizens' Forum, Netherlands, 120, 122
citizenship, 3, 4, 12, 46, 51–2, 56, 111, 114, 150–1
civil society, 45, 47, 49–51, 123, 124, 163
clean energy, 112
climate change, 12
Clinton, William Jefferson 'Bill', 110
CNN (Cable News Network), 52
coalitions, 10–11, 35, 120
cohabitation, 22
colonialism, 1, 105
Commission Nationale du débat Public, 113
common sense, 18
communism, 1, 31–2, 33, 44
Congo, 39
Conscience, Hendrik, 103
conservatism, 4, 100, 136
Constitutional Assembly, Iceland, 116, 118–19, 126–8

constitutions, 23, 48, 66, 75, 81, 84–5, 88, 91, 92, 99–102, 118, 126–30
consultation, 6, 24, 31–3, 35, 37, 107–31, 149–62, 163–4
consumerism, 4, 50
Convention on the Constitution, Ireland, 118, 128–30, 161
corruption, 2, 40, 50, 60, 134, 152, 165
Council of 500 (Boule), 59, 63, 64, 65, 67, 72, 139, 145
Croatia, 162
Crouch, Colin 51
crypto-fascism, 159
Cyprus, 159
Czechoslovakia, 102

D
D66 Party, 120
De loteling (Conscience), 103
debt, 12, 25
Declaration of the Rights of Man and of the Citizen, 88
deliberative democracy, 106–30, 149–62, 163–4
Delta Works, 12
democracy
    adversary, 107
    aleatoric-representative, 67, 77, 93, 135, 157, 160
    bi-representative, 150–62
    deliberative, 106–30, 149–62, 163–4
    direct, 24–34, 67
    distrust of, 2–16, 105, 164
    efficiency, 5–6, 10–16, 20, 24, 54, 114, 147, 158
    electoral-representative, 17, 37–57, 62, 80–105, 111, 150, 153, 157
    enthusiasm for, 1–2, 36, 47
    legitimacy, 5–10, 15, 19, 23, 24, 54, 114, 119, 122, 126, 128, 147, 148, 158
    non-electoral representative, 67
    oligarchisation of, 60, 66–7
    representative, 17, 24–37, 67, 107, 158
    unitary, 107

Democracy in America (de Tocqueville), 94–8

Democratic Fatigue Syndrome, 16, 17–57, 62, 105, 157, 159
  democracy, 17, 20–4
  electoral-representative democracy, 17, 37–57, 62
  politicians, 17–20
  representative democracy, 17, 24–37

Democratic Party, 25–7, 108

Denmark, 112–13

despotism, 5, 80

dictatorship, 5, 42, 56

Diderot, Denis, 76

diploma democracy, 19

direct democracy, 24–34, 67

distrust of democracy, 2–16, 105, 164

Dole, Robert Joseph 'Bob', 110

drawing of lots, *see* sortition

Dukakis, Michael, 106

Dupuis-Déri, Francis, 81

Dutch Republic (1581–1795), 42

E

East Germany (1949–90), 2, 58–61

East Timor, 39

Eastern Bloc, 2

economic crises, 12, 28, 44, 45, 48, 54, 118

Ecotopia (Callenbach), 134

efficiency, 5–6, 10–16, 20, 24, 54, 114, 147, 158

Egypt, 2, 27, 53

Election by Lot at Athens (Headlam), 79, 103–4

elections
  and aristocracy, 78–105, 148, 152, 160, 163
  coalitions, 10–11, 35, 120
  electoral payback, 10, 14, 16, 56, 164
  fundamentalism, 38–41, 92–3, 104
  majority principle, 119
  and media, 13–15, 16, 36, 49–54, 107, 122–3, 124, 125–6, 131, 133, 150–1, 152, 155

party membership, 9–10, 16, 164
  proportional system, 119
  reform of, 118–23, 131–62
  and restriction of democracy, 62, 78–105, 163
  vote-breaking, 35
  voter turnout, 7–8, 16, 164
  voter turnover, 8, 16

electoral payback, 10, 14, 16, 56, 164

Electoral System Citizens Forum, 162

electoral-representative democracy, 17, 37–57, 62, 80–105, 111, 150, 153, 157

Encyclopaedia (Diderot & d'Alembert), 76

enthusiasm for democracy, 1–2, 36, 47

Estonia, 162

Eurobarometer, 3

Euronews, 52

European Central Bank, 22, 28

European Citizens' Consultations, 114

European Commission, 22

European Constitution, 123

European Council, 15

European Parliament, 137–9

European Union (EU), 3–4, 9, 12, 114, 123, 133, 137–9, 158–62, 165

Eurozone crisis, 12, 21

Extremadura, Spain, 74

F

Facebook, 52, 127

Farage, Nigel, 18

fascism, 1, 31, 44, 159

Federalist Papers, 84–5, 87

Ferdinand II, King of Castile and Aragon, 74

feudalism, 42, 43, 105

financial crisis (2008), 45, 54, 118

Financial Times, 135

Finding and Keeping, 15

Finland, 9, 11, 18

Finns Party, 18

First World War (1914–18), 31, 44, 48

Fishkin, James, 106–12, 125

Five Star Movement, 35–6

Flanders, Belgium, 20, 113, 159
Flickr, 52
Florentine Republic (1115–1532), 42, 69, 70, 72, 73, 74, 75, 84
FOX, 52
France, 9, 12, 17, 23, 33, 34, 41, 42, 43, 46, 55, 62, 63, 72, 75–7, 78–83, 88–92, 94–5, 99, 100–1, 103, 113, 123, 131, 133, 136–7, 148
Frank, Thomas, 33
Frankfurt, Germany, 28–9, 73
Frankfurt Parliament (1848–9), 101
free market, 49–50, 104
freedom of association, 100
French Revolution (1789–91), 41, 43, 46, 55, 62, 63, 78–83, 88–92, 94–5, 99, 148, 159
Fukuyama, Francis, 104
fundamentalism, electoral, 38–41, 92–3, 104

G
G1000, 29
G500, 35
Gandhi, Mohandas, 106
Gataker, Thomas, 79
de Gaulle, Charles, 23
gay marriage, 130–1, 161
Genk, Netherlands, 113
Germany, 9, 12, 28–9, 31, 35, 42, 58–61, 73, 101, 112, 137
Gerona, Spain, 74
Global Corruption Barometer, 165
globalisation, 28
Golden Dawn, 18
good governance, 22
Google, 156
Grand Council (Consiglio Grande), 70–2
Greece, 9, 10, 18, 22, 26, 28, 58–67, 68, 72, 73, 74, 75–7, 79, 84, 85, 86, 87, 90, 101, 103, 108, 109, 139–40, 144, 145, 148, 150, 159
Grillo, Beppe, 17, 35
Ground Zero, New York, 113

group think, 141
Guardian, 135
Guerrero, Alex, 153
Gutenberg, Johannes, 56

H
Habermas, Jürgen, 42, 107
The Hague, Netherlands, 4
Hardt, Michael, 50
Headlam, James Wycliffe, 79, 103–4
health services, 49, 50
Hessel, Stéphane, 34
Hitler, Adolf, 31
Hofer, Norbert, 17
Honest Business (Phillips), 134
horizontality, 28, 31, 34, 57, 151, 158
House of Commons, UK, 135–6
House of Lords, UK, 135–6, 160
House of Lots, EU, 137–9
House of Peers, UK, 135
House of Representatives, US, 26, 133–5
human rights, 38, 104
Hungary, 18, 102, 159

I
Iceland, 116, 118–19, 126–8, 161
imborsazione (insertion), 69, 72, 74
Independent, 135
Indignados, 28, 30–1, 34
Indignez-vous (Hessel), 34
individualism, 4, 52, 123
Industrial Workers of the World (IWW), 33–4
infrastructure projects, 12
insaculación, 69, 74
Instagram, 52
Instituut Samenleving en Technology, 113
Interest Panels, 142, 144, 145, 147, 161
International Herald Tribune, 127
International Monetary Fund (IMF), 22
international treaties, 12
Internet, 29, 45, 47, 52–4, 56, 127, 150–1, 152
Iowa, United States, 107

Iran, 101
Iraq, 25, 39
Ireland, 9, 11, 116, 118–19, 123, 128–30, 150, 161
Italy, 9, 10, 17, 22, 23, 31, 35–6, 51, 70, 159
Ivrea, Italy, 73

J
Japan, 112
Jefferson, Thomas, 85–6
Jobbik, 18
Journal of Public Deliberation, 138
juries, 60, 64, 89, 92, 95, 97–8, 113, 122, 134, 145–6, 152, 155

K
Kanne, Peter, 4, 125
King's College, Cambridge, 103
kleroterion, 64, 68
Kosovo, 23

L
Le Pen, Marine, 17
legitimacy, 5–10, 15, 19, 23, 24, 54, 114, 119, 122, 126, 128, 147, 148, 158
Lenin, Vladimir, 31–2
Lincoln, Abraham, 104
literacy, 106, 150
Lithuania, 138
Lleida, Spain, 74
London School of Economics, 29
London Stock Exchange, 28
Lucca, Italy, 73
Luxembourg, 101

M
Madison, James, 81, 84–5, 86–7, 88
Madrid, Spain, 27, 30, 32
magistracies (arkhai), 63, 65, 67
majority principle, 119
Malta, 138
La Mancha, Spain, 74
Manchester, England, 113
Manin, Bernard, 62–3

Mansbridge, Jane, 107
Marat, Jean-Paul, 92
marketing, 19
Marx, Karl, 32
MasterCard, 134
media, 13–15, 16, 36, 43–54, 107, 122–3, 124, 125–6, 131, 133, 150–1, 152, 155
Meeting of the Minds, 114
Middle Ages, 42, 56, 70
migration, 12
military sortition, 102–3
Mill, John Stuart, 131
Minoa, 58
monarchy, 80, 100
Montesquieu, 75–6, 78, 80, 82
Monti, Mario, 22, 23
Mubarak, Hosni, 53
multinational corporations, 12
Munich, Germany, 29
Murcia, Spain, 74
Mussolini, Benito, 31

N
Nantes, France, 12
Napoleon I, Emperor of the French, 72
National Congress of Belgium, 99–100
national debt, 12, 25
national gut feeling, 18
National Issues Convention, 110
nationalism, 4
neo-liberalism, 49–50, 104
neo-parliamentarians, 35–6
Netherlands, 4, 7–8, 9, 10, 11, 12, 13–15, 17, 20, 34, 35, 48, 57, 99, 101, 113, 115, 117, 118, 120–3, 126, 159, 162
Neue Mitte, 22
New Cambridge Modern History, The, 102
New Hampshire, United States, 107
New York, United States, 24–8, 30, 32, 84–5, 113
New York Packet, The, 87
newspapers, 43, 46, 54
nominati, 73
non-electoral representative democracy, 67

Northern Ireland, 112, 129
Norway, 9
Novara Italy, 70
nuclear waste, 29

O
Obama, Barack, 25
Occupy Wall Street, 26–8, 30–1, 32–4
Of the Nature and Use of Lots (Gataker),
    79
offshore fraud, 12
oligarchy, 5, 60, 66, 67, 70, 86
ombudsman, 164
Ontario, Canada, 117, 118, 121, 122, 123
openDemocracy, 135
Orvieto, Italy, 73
Ostend, Belgium, 7
Ottoman Empire (1299–1923), 101
overpopulation, 12
Oversight Council, 143, 146, 155, 161

P
Papadimos, Loukas, 22
Paris Commune (1871), 32
parliaments, 2, 3, 8, 13–15, 19–20, 24,
    30–4, 35, 46–9, 54, 132 62, 165
    anti-parliamentarianism, 30–4, 35, 36,
        45, 48, 54, 158, 165
    coalitions, 10–11, 35, 120
    neo-parliamentarians, 35–6
    and sortition, 132–62
Parma, Italy, 73
participedia.net, 113
particracy, 38
party membership, 9–10, 16, 164
PBS (Public Broadcasting Service), 110
People's Assembly (Ekklesia), 59, 60, 63,
    64, 65, 67, 139, 140
People's Court (Heliaia), 59, 60, 63, 64,
    65, 67, 139, 144
people's mic, 27–8
People's Parliament, The, 125–6
Pericles, 59, 61
Perugia, Italy, 73

Phillips, Michael, 133
Piedmont-Sardinia (1324–1861), 101
Pinterest, 52
Pirate Party, 29, 35
Pisa, Italy, 70
Pistoia, Italy, 73
Planungszellen (planning booths), 112,
    114
Poland, 102
Policy Jury, 143, 145–6, 148
political agoraphobia, 89, 164
political talk shows, 14
politicians
    political parties, 2, 3, 9–11, 14, 16–20,
        23, 25–7, 31, 35, 37, 43–5, 47–8, 50,
        54, 56, 119, 122, 124, 125
    careerism, 17, 19–20, 66
    coalitions, 10–11, 35, 120
    distrust of citizens, 125
    and electoral payback, 10, 14, 16, 56,
        164
    emergence of, 43, 48
    financing, 11, 37, 50, 107
    membership, 9–10, 16, 45, 54, 164
    as out of touch, 17–19
    populism, 17–20, 24, 30, 33, 35, 45, 54,
        157, 159, 164–5
Porto Alegre, Brazil, 113
Portugal, 9, 159, 162
post-democracy, 51, 159
post-political thinking, 22
powerlessness, 12
press freedom, 47, 54, 100
Principles of Representative Government,
    The (Manin), 62–3
Principles of Solidarity, 28
printing press, 56, 150
professional citizens, 114
proportional system, 119
proto-democratic institutions, 40
Prussia (1525–1947), 101
Public Perspective, 110
public sphere, 42–6, 49
Puerta del Sol, Madrid, 27

R

rating bureaux, 12
Rawls, John, 107
Real Democracy Now, 28
referendums, 38, 121–4, 127, 128, 130, 164
Reflections on the Revolution in France
(Burke), 89–91
reform of democracy, 118–23, 131–62
Renaissance, 46, 56, 63, 68, 75, 93
representative democracy, 17, 24–37, 67,
107, 158
Representative House, 133–5
Republican Party, 25–7, 108
republicanism, 80–98
restriction of democracy, 62, 78–105,
163
Review Panels, 142, 145, 146, 155, 161
Robespierre, Maximilien, 91
Roma, 112
Romania, 101
Rome, Ancient (509 BC–395 AD), 60,
68, 70
Rosanvallon, Pierre, 33
rotation, 61, 68, 69, 74, 90
Rotmans, Jan, 57
Rotterdam, Netherlands, 113
Rousseau, Jean-Jacques, 47, 76–7, 90, 93
Rudd, Kevin, 115
Rules Council, 143, 146–7, 155, 161
Russia, 162

S

San Marino, 75
Saxony, Kingdom of (1806–1918), 101
Schecter, David, 140, 149
Schinkel, Willem, 34
Scotland, 123
Second World War (1939–45), 1, 31, 44,
49, 55
self-learning system, 147
self-selection, 68, 76, 114–15, 120–1
senates, 76, 100, 135, 160
    House of Lords, UK, 135–6, 160
    Sénat, France, 136

Senate, Belgium, 159–61
Senate, US, 26, 134, 160
Seven Laws of Money, The (Phillips), 134
Siena, Italy, 73
Sieyès, Emmanuel Joseph, 89
Signoria, 72
Sintomer, Yves, 136
slavery, 82, 86
Slovenia, 33
Social Contract (Rousseau), 78
social media, 45, 47, 52–4, 56, 127, 150–1,
152
socialism, 48, 103
sortition, 60–80, 82, 86, 90, 92, 93, 95,
102–3, 105, 108, 109, 112–14, 120–1,
126, 128, 131–62, 163
Southwestern Bell, 110
sovereign rulers, 42–3, 80
Soviet Union (1922–91), 33
Spain, 9, 10, 27, 28, 30, 32, 69, 73–4,
101, 159
Sparta, 58, 66
Spirit of the Laws, The (Montesquieu),
75–6, 78
St Mark's Basilica, Venice, 71
State and Revolution (Lenin), 32
state health services, 49, 50
Stealth Democracy (Hibbing & Theiss-
Morse), 21
Stembreker, 35
Stjórnlagaþing á Íslandi, 116, 118–19, 126–8
Strong Democracy (Barber), 107
strong leaders, 2
Stuttgart, Germany, 12, 28
Sutherland, Keith, 136
Sweden, 8, 9, 29, 35
Swiss Confederation (1815–48), 101
Switzerland, 9, 101
Syntagma Square, Athens, 28

T

Tahrir Square, Cairo, 27
talk shows, 14
Tea Party, 25

teaching, 14

technocracy, 21–4, 25, 30, 35, 45, 54, 87, 157, 165

Teknologi-rådet, 112

Texas, United States, 110, 112

TGV network, 12

Third House, France, 136–7

Third Way, 22

Thoughts on Government (Adams), 83–4

Time, 29

TINA (there is no alternative), 22

Tischgemeinschaften, 42

Tobback family, 20

de Tocqueville, Alexis, 93–8, 102

top-down systems, 57, 125

topicality, 53

totalitarianism, 5, 31, 48

trade unions, 31, 49, 50, 128

traffic safety, 144

transparency, 37, 127, 162

Transparency International, 165

trial by jury, *see under* juries

True Finns, 18

Trump, Donald, 18

Tumblr, 52

Tunisia, 2, 53

Turkey, 101

Twitter, 52, 127

U

unitary democracy, 107

United Kingdom, 9, 11, 18, 42, 46, 48, 51, 82, 89–91, 109, 112, 113, 119, 123, 125–6, 129, 132, 135–6, 137, 139, 159, 160

United Kingdom Independence Party (UKIP), 18

United States, 12, 18, 21, 24–8, 30, 32, 41, 43, 46, 50, 55, 62, 63, 78–88, 93–8, 104, 106–12, 113, 122, 132, 133–5, 137, 148

Universal Declaration of Human Rights (1948), 38, 104

universal suffrage, 38, 43, 47

University College Dublin, 129

University of Exeter, 136

University of Texas, 107

V

Van Doorn, Jacobus Adrianus Antonius, 19

Van Parijs, Philippe, 131

Van Rompuy, Herman, 15

Venetian Republic (697–1797), 42, 68, 70–2, 73, 75

Verdin, 58–62, 67

Vermont, United States, 138

Vicenza, Italy, 70

voting
    turnout, 7–8, 16, 164
    turnover, 8, 16
    vote-breaking, 35

W

Wallonia, Belgium, 159

We the Citizens project, 129

Wenling, Zhejiang, 113

What is the Third Estate? (Sieyès), 89

Wilders, Geert, 17

Wir sind das Volk, 59

women's suffrage, 131, 154

workers' rights, 102, 154, 165

World Bank, 22

World Values Survey, 1–2

Wutbürger, 28–9

Y

Year of Citizens, 114, 158

Young Turk Revolution (1908), 101

Z

Zaragoza, Spain, 74

Žižek, Slavoj, 33

Zuccotti Park, New York, 27, 32

DAVID VAN REYBROUCK is considered "one of the leading intellectuals in Europe" (Der Tagesspiegel) and is a pioneering advocate of participatory democracy. He founded the G1000 Citizens' Summit, and his work has led to trials in participatory democracy throughout Belgium and Holland. He is also one of the most highly regarded literary and political writers of his generation, whose most recent book, *Congo: The Epic History of a People*, won 19 prizes, sold 500,000 copies, and has been translated into a dozen languages. It was described as a "masterpiece" by the *Independent* and "magnificent" by *The New York Times*.

After finishing her studies at the University of Manchester, translator LIZ WATERS worked for some years with English-language texts and at a literary agency in Amsterdam before becoming a full-time translator of literary fiction and nonfiction. Authors whose books she has translated include Lieve Joris, Jaap Scholten, Luuk van Middelaar, Douwe Draaisma, and Geert Mak.

KOFI ANNAN is a Nobel Peace Prize laureate and was Secretary-General of the United Nations between 1997 and 2006.

ABOUT SEVEN STORIES PRESS

Seven Stories Press is an independent book publisher based in New York City. We publish works of the imagination by such writers as Nelson Algren, Russell Banks, Octavia E. Butler, Ani DiFranco, Assia Djebar, Ariel Dorfman, Coco Fusco, Barry Gifford, Martha Long, Luis Negrón, Peter Plate, Hwang Sok-yong, Lee Stringer, and Kurt Vonnegut, to name a few, together with political titles by voices of conscience, including Subhankar Banerjee, the Boston Women's Health Collective, Noam Chomsky, Angela Y. Davis, Human Rights Watch, Derrick Jensen, Ralph Nader, Loretta Napoleoni, Gary Null, Greg Palast, Project Censored, Barbara Seaman, Alice Walker, Gary Webb, and Howard Zinn, among many others. Seven Stories Press believes publishers have a special responsibility to defend free speech and human rights, and to celebrate the gifts of the human imagination, wherever we can. In 2012 we launched Triangle Square books for young readers with strong social justice and narrative components, telling personal stories of courage and commitment. For additional information, visit www.sevenstories.com.